"Ruth Schwenk and Karen Ehman have done it again—and those of us who love their devotionals are better for it! *Trusting God in All the Things* won't just bless you for the five minutes you spend reading it each morning; these daily Scriptures and stories will continue to resonate with you throughout your day. This devotional will help you live devoted in the midst of 'All the Things.'"

—Wendy Speake, author of *Triggers* and *The 40-Day Sugar Fast*

"Karen and Ruth are wildly gifted at speaking life-giving truth + grace over the things that weigh heavy on our hearts and tempt us to worry that God has forgotten or forsaken us. *Trusting God in All the Things* is an invitation and a tool to connect with Jesus and experience the peace that passes all understanding in His presence!"

—Jeannie Cunnion, author of *Don't Miss Out*

"When we face hard stuff, we always need those friends like Karen Ehman and Ruth Schwenk, who hold us up and cheer us on. In their newest devotional, *Trusting God in All the Things*, they walk alongside you and, most important, they point you to the real source of hope—Jesus. With depth, wisdom, and practical advice, this devotional is a must-read on your journey!"

—Alli Worthington, author of *Standing Strong*

"Ruth Schwenk and Karen Ehman are the friends we all need to help us get through the days and weeks and months that just feel overwhelming. I absolutely love this devotional because it is so simple to read but makes you feel like you just walked away from a really valuable conversation—one that leads you closer to the heart of God no matter how hard it feels to trust Him. This devotional is a must-have, and you will use it again and again! Each day's reading will make your heart feel a little lighter and each hard thing in front of you a little more doable."

—Nicki Koziarz, bestselling author and speaker

"Don't let the bite-sized chapters fool you; there is *power* in these pages! With the Scripture verses and prayer prompts bracketing each day's devotion, you'll find purpose and peace in the midst of loneliness, anxiety, broken relationships, and much more. *Trusting God in All the Things* is one of those books you'll return to again and again—keep a copy in your car, your purse, your bedside table, wherever you need to meet God in the middle minutes of your day!"

—Jodie Berndt, author of the bestselling *Praying the Scriptures* series

"What a wonderful encouragement this devotional is! This book reads like a letter from a compassionate friend. Karen and Ruth write from personal experience and remind us that God sees our needs and cares deeply for us. Over and over, their biblical wisdom and encouragement leads to reflection, rest, and freedom. If you feel anxious, overwhelmed, or alone, this book is for you. *Trusting God in All the Things* is a comforting balm for the soul."

—Courtney Joseph, author and blogger at WomenLivingWell.org

"*Trusting God in All the Things* keeps things real! I can always count on Karen Ehman and Ruth Schwenk to understand my everyday needs and offer just the right encouragement my heart longs for. Each day, I feel more surefooted in my faith and in my trust in God as I read their godly wisdom."

—Amber Lia, bestselling coauthor of the *Triggers* book series

"When I'm reading a devotional, I want to know that the writer is sharing not only their highlight reel, but their middle seasons too. Ruth and Karen share exactly those types of moments with grace, hope, and faith to encourage and grow the faith of their readers while sharing biblical wisdom."

—Melissa Mulvaney, Canton, Michigan

"Who hasn't ever wondered if God can truly be trusted? I was blessed by the depth of wisdom Karen and Ruth offered in these short daily readings. Their words coupled with God's Word fed and fortified my heart. I highlighted. I bookmarked. I walked away with hope-filled reasons to trust."

—Kimberly Henderson, Inman, South Carolina

"If you're looking for hope in the mundane, in the waiting, or in the midst of suffering, I believe you will find it here. Each story, each devotional, is like a little glimpse of hope filling you up again and guiding you back to the source of our hope: Jesus."

—Jessi Schafer, St. Johns, Michigan

TRUSTING
GOD
— IN —
ALL *the* THINGS

TRUSTING
GOD
— IN —
ALL *the* THINGS

90 Devotions for Finding
Peace in Your Every Day

Karen Ehman and Ruth Schwenk

BETHANYHOUSE

a division of Baker Publishing Group
Minneapolis, Minnesota

© 2022 by Karen Ehman and Ruth Schwenk

Published by Bethany House Publishers
11400 Hampshire Avenue South
Minneapolis, Minnesota 55438
www.bethanyhouse.com

Bethany House Publishers is a division of
Baker Publishing Group, Grand Rapids, Michigan

Printed in the United States of America

Library of Congress Cataloging-in-Publication Data
Names: Ehman, Karen, author. | Schwenk, Ruth, author.
Title: Trusting God in all the things : 90 devotions for finding peace in your
    every day / Karen Ehman and Ruth Schwenk.
Description: Minneapolis, Minnesota : Bethany House Publishers, a division of
    Baker Publishing Group, [2022] | Includes bibliographical references.
Identifiers: LCCN 2021046296 | ISBN 9780764239618 (cloth) | ISBN
    9781493435784 (ebook)
Subjects: LCSH: Trust in God—Christianity—Prayers and devotions.
Classification: LCC BV4637 .E36 2022 | DDC 234/.23—dc23
LC record available at https://lccn.loc.gov/2021046296

Unless otherwise indicated, Scripture quotations are from the Holy Bible, New International Version®. NIV®. Copyright © 1973, 1978, 1984, 2011 by Biblica, Inc.™ Used by permission of Zondervan. All rights reserved worldwide. www.zondervan.com. The "NIV" and "New International Version" are trademarks registered in the United States Patent and Trademark Office by Biblica, Inc.™

Scripture quotations identified AMP are from the Amplified® Bible (AMP), copyright © 2015 by The Lockman Foundation. Used by permission. www.Lockman.org

Scripture quotations identified CSB have been taken from the Christian Standard Bible®, copyright © 2017 by Holman Bible Publishers. Used by permission. Christian Standard Bible® and CSB® are federally registered trademarks of Holman Bible Publishers.

Scripture quotations identified ESV are from The Holy Bible, English Standard Version® (ESV®), copyright © 2001 by Crossway, a publishing ministry of Good News Publishers. Used by permission. All rights reserved. ESV Text Edition: 2016

Scripture quotations identified KJV are from the King James Version of the Bible.

Scripture quotations identified NKJV are from the New King James Version®. Copyright © 1982 by Thomas Nelson. Used by permission. All rights reserved.

Scripture quotations identified NLT are from the Holy Bible, New Living Translation, copyright © 1996, 2004, 2007, 2013, 2015 by Tyndale House Foundation. Used by permission of Tyndale House Publishers, Inc., Carol Stream, Illinois 60188. All rights reserved.

Cover design by Emily Weigel
Cover floral illustration by Love-Lava
Interior design by Sarah Asprec

Karen Ehman and Ruth Schwenk are represented by Meredith Brock.

Baker Publishing Group publications use paper produced from sustainable forestry practices and post-consumer waste whenever possible.

22 23 24 25 26 27 28   7 6 5 4 3 2 1

To you, our precious readers.
May you discover peace and experience calm
as you learn to trust God in every area of life.

CONTENTS

Contents

Contents

Contents

INTRODUCTION

Hey, friend. We see you there. You're trying your absolute best to do all the things, spending much of your time keeping connected with all your people. As you constantly toggle between your responsibilities and relationships, it often leaves little time for yourself—or for connecting with Jesus. This can create a feeling of anxiousness in your mind and hurry in your soul. Your heart desperately longs for calm amidst your clamoring duties, stacked schedule, and life's unexpected circumstances.

The *Cambridge English Dictionary* defines *calm* as "peaceful, quiet, and without worry," and also as, "without hurried movement or noise."[1] To obtain a heart that is indicative of the first definition—peaceful, quiet, and without worry—we need moments described by the second definition—unhurried, still, and devoid of noise.

What our overwhelmed hearts need is true calm—a calm that can only come from God himself. To obtain it, we must pursue a daily connection with God, which we pray this devotional will provide. More than success, time management skills, or people's praise, our hearts need a refreshing encounter with God each day. We can learn to carve out time to connect our hearts with God's heart, time to experience God's love, grow in his grace, and explore his truth. As we do, we learn to follow and serve God with a sense of purpose and experience the calm we all crave no matter what we are facing.

It is our deepest desire and most sincere prayer that the devotional entries within this book will point you to the Author of life himself.

Drink in the scriptural truths presented. Ponder the questions posed. Take time to earnestly pray from your heart. But most of all, expect the Lord to be ever close as you do, empowering you through the Holy Spirit to trust him in every area of your life.

We are praying for you. May you find the peace and calm that only Jesus can provide, trusting God in all the things. He is always faithful to meet you, strengthen you, and draw you closer to him.

In His Great Love,

Karen and Ruth

1 | Even Jesus Was Overwhelmed

Ruth

Scripture to Study

And being in anguish, he prayed more earnestly, and his sweat was like drops of blood falling to the ground.

Luke 22:44

What has you overwhelmed right now? Is there something that seems too big for you? Stress can feel like an invisible press we're caught in. A weight. Or a trap that is slowly squeezing the life out of us!

I felt it with every miscarriage. It reared its ugly head and tightened its clutches when my husband was diagnosed with cancer. I felt it when our son was applying for college. We've all felt the overwhelming pressing and squeezing of life's circumstances.

And so it might encourage you, as it did me, to be reminded that even Jesus was overwhelmed. He, too, felt the suffocating and exhausting effects of stress leading up to his death on the cross. Shortly before Jesus' arrest and betrayal, he withdrew to a place called the Mount of Olives (Luke 22:39). In a garden called Gethsemane, Jesus was overcome with a crushing stress.

It was there, Luke tells us, that Jesus was in "anguish" (v. 44). This was a deep and intense grief. It was an immense weight. Anticipating his death, Jesus experienced a gut-wrenching sorrow and pain almost too unbearable to handle. The mention of sweat "like drops of blood" is meant to show us that Jesus had reached the limits of his human ability to endure.

All this he suffered for us. For me. For you. And of course, for the sake of doing his Father's will. But what I don't want us to miss is that even Jesus was overcome with sorrow and anguish. He, too, knew stress. And he knows ours.

If we are not careful, we can add stress on top of our stress. We can take a difficult season or circumstance that is pushing and pulling on us and add even more weight to the already heavy burden we are carrying. How do we do this? By wrongly believing we should never be stressed or overwhelmed! This is where we need to keep coming back to Jesus. Drawing near to him. Listening to him. Remembering his own anguish. But also, being reminded of what he did *with* his anguish.

The question is not whether we will be overwhelmed, but where we will take that stress and overwhelm. To whom or what will we turn? Luke tells us that as Jesus' anguish increased, so did Jesus' prayer. He prayed "more earnestly." He didn't deny his pain or minimize his anguish, but he drew closer to his Father, who alone is the source of comfort and strength in times of trouble.

Will you do the same today? Be encouraged that Jesus knows our anguish and shows us where to take our stress, even when it feels like too much to handle.

POINTS TO PONDER

How do you find encouragement from knowing that even Jesus was in anguish or felt crushing stress?

_____

_____

_____

_____

_____

Jesus knows what we are going through. He wants us to draw close to him in our stress so that we might share in his suffering, and by doing so find the grace to endure with him and grow in greater intimacy with him. Take a moment to think through those circumstances you need to give over to him.

PAUSING TO PRAY

Father, *I need you to handle what is too heavy for me to carry. So I am surrendering to you* _____

_____

_____

_____

_____

_____

2 | You Don't Have to Crush It

Karen

I grabbed a glass of lemon mint iced tea and headed out to the front porch for a little brain break. I was feeling overwhelmed by all the responsibilities that come with the various roles I have in life as a worker, wife, mother, and daughter. And truthfully, I was certain I was not doing a decent job at any of them that day.

I had my phone with me, so I hopped on social media and began to tap, swipe, and scroll my way around. *Big mistake.*

Each click of the screen seemed to showcase to me others who were *not* struggling in work or at home. Instead, they were "crushing it," as one post declared.

Within the span of about three minutes, I was shown all the following: a woman who was remodeling her kitchen by installing trendy subway tile all by herself; a small-business owner who had doubled her profits in the last year by implementing some new marketing strategies; and a mom who posted one of those "day in the life" series in her Instagram stories detailing how she had homeschooled her children, thoroughly cleaned her home from top to bottom, written a new blog post, recorded a podcast episode, and somehow still had time to whip up some homemade sourdough bread to accompany the from-scratch meal she was preparing for company that night. *Sigh.* These sisters were crushing it, all right. I, on the other hand, was feeling my spirit crushed by comparison.

It is so easy to want to emulate others we see who seem so fruitful. After all, they must be doing something right . . . *right?* But is crushing it at home or at work what God calls us to strive for most? Should we seek accomplishments and run after success? Or is there something altogether different God wants us to chase even more?

Proverbs 21:21 encourages us to pursue righteousness and faithful love. In Hebrew, the word for *righteousness* means honesty, fairness, and just deeds. The biblical concept of faithful love denotes acts of kindness, especially to the lowly, needy, and miserable. When I think of this deeper meaning, I am reminded of the rule of life my mother taught me.

She encouraged me to stop looking at other people who seem to be better off in life than I and instead seek out the ones who surely weren't: "There is always someone out there who has things worse off than you. Go find that person and do something to make their day. In a strange way, it will end up making yours as well."

Mom was right. Showing kindness to the lonely, needy, and miserable is not only in keeping with the advice in this proverb, but also a remedy for our deflated spirits when we spy others out there crushing it. Of course, there is nothing wrong with success and hard work, nor with sharing it for others to see. However, let's strive to measure our lives instead by our pursuit of faithful love—love showered on us by God and then shown to others.

Rather than trying to "crush it," let's focus on looking for those who are crushed in spirit and doing something to cheer and encourage them.

POINT TO PONDER

How might having the goal of showing love to the lonely, needy, and miserable as your pursuit help to change your perspective today?

_____

_____

_____

_____

PAUSING TO PRAY

Gracious Father, *help me to get my eyes off others' successes and instead* _____

_____

_____

_____

_____

_____

_____

3 | You Are Not Alone

Ruth

David felt alone. He felt forsaken. Fearful for his own life, he found refuge in a secluded cave.

At least seven different times, King Saul tried to kill David. He and his men were intent on destroying him. And so it is no wonder that David, anticipating the worst, fled to a remote cave—most likely Adullam (1 Samuel 22:1).

It was in that lonely cave that David poured out his loneliness with the only One he knew would never leave him. We read this prayer in Psalm 142:4 when David cries out, "Look and see, there is no one at my right hand; no one is concerned for me. I have no refuge; no one cares for my life."

Trials can be painful, can't they? But they can also be lonely. While some people choose to walk toward us in our pain, many do not. So it is easy to feel isolated, like David. Even the best of friends have limits. They can only do so much and be so much. They can be a support to us but never fully satisfy us or save us, as God can. He alone is our "refuge." So we need to be grateful for how our friends are *able* to love us, not for how we *wish* they would love us.

But there is another detail in this story we shouldn't miss!

Trials don't always tell the full truth. In our pain, we can lose perspective. This is why it is interesting to me that in 1 Samuel 22, when

David's family and those who sympathized with him heard about his fleeing, they went to find him. And not just one or two people—about four hundred! (1 Samuel 22:1–2).

Think about that for a moment. As David is crying out, lamenting his loneliness, God is already sending an army, literally, to gather around him. Now notice how our psalm ends:

> Listen to my cry,
>   for I am in desperate need;
> rescue me from those who pursue me,
>   for they are too strong for me.
> Set me free from my prison,
>   that I may praise your name.
> Then the righteous will gather about me
>   because of your goodness to me.
>   Psalm 142:6–7

David not only learns that God alone is his refuge, but he also discovers that, while even the best of friends have limits, he was not really alone after all! So what does all of this mean for us? Most important, it means God alone is our refuge. He alone will never leave us or forsake us. But it also means that God will surround us with friends who *do* care, when we ask him. So, here is the beautiful truth you can be assured of and rest in today: You are loved and you are never alone!

POINTS TO PONDER

Why is it dangerous to focus on how you *wish* your friends would love you instead of being grateful for how they are *able* to love you?

_____

_____

_____

_____

If you are struggling with loneliness, remember that Jesus knows what it is like to feel alone, betrayed, and even forsaken. Draw near to him and don't be afraid to begin asking God for the right kind of friends to gather around you in your time of need.

PAUSING TO PRAY

Father, *help me to begin cultivating righteous friendships by*

_____

_____

_____

_____

_____

_____

4 | Not Yours!

Karen

Scripture to Study

His divine power has given us everything required for life and godliness through the knowledge of him who called us by his own glory and goodness.

2 Peter 1:3 CSB

Last week I traveled to visit our adult daughter who'd just purchased her first home, an adorable mid-century brick ranch. After a week of unpacking boxes, cleaning cupboards, and organizing closets, I packed one more item—my carry-on bag—and headed back to the airport to return home.

After a ninety-minute flight, the aircraft touched down. And as always, when opening the overhead compartment to retrieve my carry-on bag, I scrutinized it very carefully to be sure I was grabbing the correct one.

I popped open the bin and laughed at what I saw. One savvy traveler had used a white chalk marker to write two simple words on the bottom of his suitcase: "Not yours!" And it worked. No one grabbed his luggage mistakenly.

God used that humorous incident to speak to my heart that day. At that time in my life, I was wrestling with feelings of envy toward a few people in my circle of friends. My unique shade of green had established an ugly root in my heart, causing me to focus on what I lacked rather than on the blessings I did have.

Spying the phrase *Not yours!* on that suitcase was the wake-up my wandering mind needed. I needed to stop envying the lives God has given others and be satisfied with the one he has given me.

Second Peter 1:3 makes this bold statement about our lives: Everything that is required for life and godliness has already been given to us by God through his divine power. While we might not have _____ (fill in the blank with your own area of envy), we *do* have all we need to live a life of godliness.

All humans who turn their lives over to God have equal access to him. We all can study his Word, connect with him through prayer, and discover a fulfilling life serving him on earth. His unfailing love toward each of us is vast, without partiality, and never-ending.

So the next time you find yourself envious, wanting to grab what someone else has, remind yourself, *Not yours!* Instead, focus your mind on God, thanking him for the many blessings—no matter how simple—he has gifted to you.

We can choose to be content rather than waste energy wishing we resided in someone else's circumstances. Let's spend our time pursuing godliness as we deepen our walk with Jesus. Maybe we don't have what someone else does, but we do have the Lord, and he is enough.

POINTS TO PONDER

In which area of your life are you tempted to be envious of others?

_____

_____

_____

How can today's verse encourage you to focus on living a life of godliness rather than wishing you dwelt in someone else's circumstances?

_____

_____

_____

_____

PAUSING TO PRAY

Father, *I want to learn to be content despite my circumstances. Help me keep my eyes on you rather than on* _____

_____

_____

_____

_____

_____

5 | The God Who Cares

Ruth

Scripture to Study

What do you want me to do for you?

Luke 18:41

What do you need most from God right now? Imagine Jesus asking you what you want him to do for you. I suspect the answer to that question would be easy. It might seem obvious.

"Give me my marriage back, Jesus."
"I need a job."
"Keep my cancer away."
"Open my womb."

In Luke 18, we meet a man who, though he is blind, can see his need clearly. He can also see Jesus clearly. He hears about Jesus before he sees him. And we're told that as the buzz of the crowd was swirling around him, passing him by, he asks what is going on (v. 36).

The crowd tells him it's "Jesus of Nazareth." The blind man sees Jesus more clearly than the crowds do. How do we know this? Because when he calls out to Jesus, he doesn't call him "Jesus of Nazareth"; he calls him "Son of David" (vv. 38–39).

The blind man knows exactly who Jesus is! He is the long-awaited Messiah. He is the Savior, not only of Israel, but of the whole world. He is the One the Jewish people had been waiting for. The One who would come to begin setting the world right. The One who had come to "proclaim good news to the poor," the One who had come to "proclaim freedom for the prisoners." This Jesus had come to recover "sight for the blind" and "set the oppressed free" (Luke 4:18). And ultimately, this Jesus had come to die that we might live (John 3:16).

Jesus is not only powerful, but he is also compassionate. "Have mercy on me," the blind man begs (v. 39). It's stunning, isn't it, that Jesus turns to him and asks the question, "What do you want me to do for you?"

Imagine Jesus asking you that very question today. He loves *you*. He is for *you*. He has mercy toward *you*. Just as Jesus asked the blind man, he is asking you, "What do you want me to do for you?" Don't be afraid to answer Jesus. Set aside your doubts. And simply answer him. Present to him your greatest need. You can trust him.

POINTS TO PONDER

Why is it so difficult to believe that Jesus really wants to help you?

_____

_____

_____

Jesus not only has the power to help, but he also has the heart to help. While he may not always give us what we want when we feel we need it and in the way we think he should, he is the God who cares for us. And he invites us to humbly tell him what we need. What are the things you are struggling to give over to him today?

_____

_____

_____

_____

_____

PAUSING TO PRAY

Jesus, you came to reveal the heart of God the Father to us—a God who cares deeply for us. You know what I need. No matter what your response is, I love you and trust you. But out of your mercy, would you _____

_____

_____

_____

_____

_____

---

6 | You Have All That You Need

Karen

Scripture to Study

The LORD is my shepherd; I have all that I need.

Psalm 23:1 NLT

The bell rang at 3:30 p.m. on the final day of school for my third-grade year. I was extra thrilled because I was going to do something that summer I'd never done before: head off to summer camp for an entire week! This camp in the Michigan countryside boasted adventurous walking trails and rustic cabins that reminded me of something out of a Laura Ingalls Wilder book about prairie life I'd just read in English class.

My mom and I pulled out the packing list the campground had mailed us. Many items made sense to me such as a toothbrush, pajamas, and bug spray. But others were a little puzzling to my third-grade mind. Why did I need two large garbage bags, a gallon-size ziplock bag, a clean half-gallon milk carton, and a photograph of my family?

It wasn't until certain points in the camp week that I discovered the uses for the mystery items. One garbage bag was to place my dirty clothes in before putting them back in my suitcase. The other served as a barrier beneath my sleeping bag the one night we got to sleep outside under the stars. A wet bathing suit fit perfectly in the ziplock bag, making the trip home in my suitcase without getting everything else soaked. And finally, the milk carton and photograph of my family turned into a lovely paperweight during craft class. While I had no clue I would need these items, the camp director knew exactly what the week entailed, so she wanted to make sure I was properly equipped.

Psalm 23 has been a go-to psalm for so many people through the ages. It comforts us in times of sorrow. It strengthens us when we are afraid.

But recently when I was reading it, one phrase jumped out at me as it never had before: *I have all that I need.*

Our loving heavenly Father—the Director of our days—knows precisely what lies ahead. We are promised that we will not be found lacking. The Lord knows exactly what we need. At those times when we look around at others—wishing we had their circumstances, their financial status, their job, or even their people—we must train our brains to instead look to Christ. He knows exactly what we need—and just when we will need it.

Just as a shepherd tends carefully to his sheep, God is watching over us, ready to feed our souls and care for us physically. There is not a single place where we are out of his reach. As the psalmist David says in the last verse of this psalm,

> Surely your goodness and unfailing love will pursue me all the days of my life.

> (v. 6 NLT)

Quiet your heart today, trusting in the God who knows exactly what lies ahead. He will make sure you have all that you need.

POINTS TO PONDER

How is your anxiety level when it comes to the future? Circle a number below, with 1 signifying having complete trust and faith in God and 10 representing being highly anxious.

1   2   3   4   5   6   7   8   9   10

What can you remind yourself of from Psalm 23:1 to help that number change?

_____

_____

_____

PAUSING TO PRAY

Father, I want to trust that you have already provided me with all that I need. Remind me that _____

_____

_____

_____

_____

_____

7 | Living Calm

Ruth

Scripture to Study

Jesus was in the stern, sleeping on a cushion. The disciples woke him and said to him, "Teacher, don't you care if we drown?"

Mark 4:38

saw my phone light up and immediately recognized the number. My thoughts immediately went wild!

Why would they be calling me?
Is something wrong?
Do they know something I don't?

It was my doctor's office. And before I had any answers, I had at least ten different assumptions! All of which turned out to be wrong, as it was simply a reminder of an upcoming appointment.

No crisis, just a call. But it still left me feeling a bit chaotic. It took a bit of time to mop up the mess my mind left behind.

When my thoughts finally cooled down, I began to think about the time Jesus took his disciples out in the middle of the lake. It was there, far from the shores and safety, that a storm swirled around them—a real storm. Dangerous. And potentially deadly.

Mark's gospel tells us something interesting. The disciples were in a complete state of panic. Chaos swirled around them and in them. Yet Jesus, who was with them and who had said they were going to the other side, was sound asleep. Jesus was not moved by the chaos. He was Lord over it.

In Mark 4:38 we read, "Jesus was in the stern, sleeping on a cushion. The disciples woke him and said to him, 'Teacher, don't you care if we drown?'"

Imagine living with that kind of calm. The conviction that God really is in control. That he is with us. And that there is nothing that passes into our life that doesn't first pass through his love. Wouldn't it cultivate in us calm instead of chaos? Wouldn't it grow in us the fruit of faith, hope, and love?

Friend, whatever you are facing today, be reminded that Jesus really is with you. May his presence bring you peace. And may his companionship replace your chaos with an unexplainable calm.

POINTS TO PONDER

What does it look like to be calm in the face of chaos?

_____

_____

_____

There are no emergencies in heaven. God is not caught off guard by what we are going through. Is there a particular situation that has you feeling frantic? Ask God to help you turn that over to him. He is in complete control.

PAUSING TO PRAY

Father, I surrender the chaos of _____

_____

_____

_____

8 | A Sermonette for Your Soul

Karen

Scripture to Study

Why are you cast down, O my soul,
and why are you in turmoil within me?

Psalm 42:5 ESV

Our young adult son, Spencer, recently went on a three-month backpacking trip. His plan was to visit fourteen state and national parks, camping out in the wilderness . . . wait for it . . . all alone! Well, that is except for the many bears, mountain lions, snakes, and other wild creatures my internet searches confirmed could possibly be accompanying him.

It filled my mama-heart with dread, and my mind raced with worry when I thought about what danger he might encounter—not only in sharing the terrain with wildlife, but also the varying weather elements he'd be exposed to when stretching out under the stars to sleep each night.

In times of worry—whether I am concerned about a loved one or anxious about something affecting only myself—I have often camped out in the book of Psalms, searching for a passage that would help calm my fearful soul. In many of the emotion-saturated psalms, we can eavesdrop as the writer pours out his uneasy, apprehensive thoughts to a God who always bends close enough to hear our deepest cries.

Psalm 42 is one of several pieces penned by the Sons of Korah (Psalms 42, 44–49, 84–85, 87–88). It is a psalm of lament—a heart cry to God during a dire situation. It is both a raw display of emotion and an honest plea for divine action.

We read in this psalm the expression "O my soul." The word translated as *soul* here is a Hebrew noun that can mean living being, self, or seat of human emotions and passions.[1] When the phrase O *my soul* dots the landscape of other psalms, it indicates a conflict in the writer's mind, perhaps even a slight panic arising in his heart. He is trying to control his runaway emotions by preaching to his own soul.

With the next soul-searching phrase comes the answer to the psalmist's dilemma: "My soul is cast down within me; therefore I remember you" (Psalm 42:6). This act of remembering allows him to control his soul, trusting in God and his goodness.

When we experience worry, apprehension, and at times even fright, turning our thoughts away from our racing emotions and fixating them instead upon the immovable God can help calm our hearts and soothe our souls. This is the thinking I had to follow when my son was out in the wilderness. (And, by the way, he returned home safely, having experienced only a somewhat close call with a mountain lion who thankfully decided to find his supper elsewhere!)

When we find ourselves rattled emotionally, we can learn to preach a short sermon to ourselves: *Remember God*. It worked for the psalmist. It worked for me when my son was wandering the countryside, and it can work for you too.

As we learn to align our thoughts with Scripture and remember the goodness of God, we can trust our loving God in all things and not fear the outcome of whatever situation we face.

POINTS TO PONDER

Can you remember a time of turmoil when you had to learn to speak truth to your soul by recalling the goodness of God?

_____

_____

_____

_____

PAUSING TO PRAY

Father, *when my soul becomes rattled, help me to remember your character and your righteous actions to me in the past. I choose today to* _____

_____

_____

_____

_____

_____

9 | You Are the One Jesus Loves

Ruth

Scripture to Study

Lord, the one you love is sick.

John 11:3

We don't know a lot about Jesus' relationship with Mary and Martha and their brother, Lazarus, but we do know that he knew them well and loved them a lot. This makes Jesus' initial response to the statement above all the more peculiar.

Lazarus had fallen ill, and his sisters, Mary and Martha, sent word to Jesus to come help. Their cry is simple. Straight to the point. And urgent.

"Lord, the one you love is sick," they said.

I can't help but notice that they don't appeal to Jesus' power. They don't even ask for a miracle. They simply appeal to Jesus' *love*. Why? Because they know that whoever Jesus loves is the person Jesus will not abandon.

You would expect that someone Jesus deeply loves is someone whom Jesus would quickly rescue. But this is not what he does. Just a few verses later, after hearing about Lazarus, we're told that "he stayed where he was two more days, and then he said to his disciples, 'Let us go back to Judea'" (John 11:6–7).

Two more days? Those must have been two of the longest days for Mary and Martha.

Have you ever felt as though God was taking too much time? Maybe you've felt he was slow to respond. Jesus had his reasons, but Mary and Martha probably had their doubts: *Does he really love Lazarus? Does he really love us? Why isn't he doing something right now?*

There is a lesson in this for each of us too. We must never make the mistake of thinking that God's love and our suffering are incompatible.

Our comfort, or lack thereof, is not commentary on God's character. Suffering and pain and hurt are not contradictions of God's love.

One thing we can be sure of is that when we weep, when we experience loss or pain, it is not because of a lack of God's love. We need the reminder that God is not only present with us but that he loves us. And he will not abandon us.

Will you love Jesus even when you don't understand what he is doing? Will you love him when it hurts? And when you are scared? He loved us in his suffering and he has promised to never leave us in ours (Romans 8:38–39).

POINTS TO PONDER

What temptation do you need to avoid while you wait on God's timing?

_____

Our suffering is not incompatible with God's love. And his timing is not always ours. So be patient as you wait for him to show his love in his perfect timing. Write down a few things you are waiting on him for and commit to handing those over to him. Be sure to put the date so you can look back and remember.

_____

_____

_____

PAUSING TO PRAY

Father, I am the one you love. My trials do not tell the truth about who you are or what you will do. I will wait on you by _____

_____

10 | The Uttered and the Unspoken

Karen

Scripture to Study

You have given him his heart's desire
and have not withheld the request of his lips.
Selah

Psalm 21:2 ESV

I once had a friend in high school who had a funny little way of talking about herself: She often did so in the third person. After class, if she had a craving for some fries and a root beer float, she'd say, "I do think Colleen could go for some delightful A&W cuisine right about now. What say you?"

In Psalm 21, we see the shepherd boy turned king, David, speaking of himself in the third person as he displays his gratitude to God for granting him victory over an adversarial king and his kingdom. He doesn't hog the glory for the triumph. Instead, he gives credit where credit is due. He declares that it is the Lord's immense power—not his own—that brought him salvation in the heat of the battle.

This psalm is often referred to as one of the *royal psalms*. This grouping of psalms (Psalms 2; 18; 20; 21; 45; 72; 89; 101; 110) is labeled as royal because the subject matter of each involves the king of Israel and his military excursions. In this psalm full of thanksgiving, David is grateful for God's answering his spoken requests as well as God's granting his unspoken longings—the desires of his heart.

Because David knows that the victory was not due to his own power, skill, or military might but rather the faithfulness and immeasurable strength of the Lord, David is confident God would continue to cause him to reign securely on the throne (Psalm 21:7).

We also face battles. Of course, they aren't usually filled with physical combat, with bows shooting arrows toward us. However, in the heat of our conflicts, we offer both spoken requests of the lips—our prayers—and also those silent longings of our souls—the desires of our hearts. What an encouragement to us to know that God hears both manners of crying for help. Whether we articulate out loud, or silently plead with words that are not audibly expressed, God always hears.

What prayer requests have you been saying out loud lately? Have you shared them with a friend or offered them up in your small group? How about those areas of concern you keep tucked away in your heart, the ones only the Lord knows about?

Jesus, the ultimate Davidic King and one true Messiah, stands waiting to hear both modes of messaging. He can grant us success in the spiritual battles we face, crowning us with spiritual victory according to his will.

Whether uttered or unspoken, the God of the universe cares about the concerns in your heart. Take them to him today.

POINTS TO PONDER

Which do you need a reply from God about, your spoken requests or the silent desires of your heart? Remember, God knows them both!

_____

_____

_____

PAUSING TO PRAY

Father, I praise you for the victory you granted David in his battles. Thank you for offering me the same help and for _____

_____

_____

11 | Be Watchful

Ruth

Scripture to Study

Watch and pray so that you will not fall into temptation. The spirit is willing, but the flesh is weak.

Mark 14:38

I tiptoed around the corner, walking as slowly and as softly as I could. All I wanted to do was get from the kitchen to our bathroom. You'd think our home, of all places, would be the safest and most comfortable space. But not when your kids are going through that stage when all they want to do is jump out and scare you. Then, no place was safe. They would hide around a corner. Jump out of a closet. Grab your ankle from under the couch. And so, with every step, wherever I went, I was watchful. Fortunately, our children have finally outgrown this phase!

But there is a different kind of watchfulness we are called to, isn't there? And it is not a phase, because our spiritual adversary never outgrows, gives up on, or wearies of "looking for someone to devour" (1 Peter 5:8).

We are not called to walk through life scared, but we are called to walk through life wisely. We are encouraged to have an alertness—one that Jesus tells us is necessary if we are to stay alive spiritually. In Mark 14, shortly before Jesus' arrest, he gets away with Peter, James, and John—that inner circle of disciples. Earlier, they had been given a glimpse of his glory; now they would get a glimpse of his agony.

"Watch and pray," he tells them, "so that you will not fall into temptation" (Mark 14:38). Three times in this chapter we're told Jesus went away to be alone with his Father, and three times he returned to find his closest disciples asleep. Not alert. Certainly not watching.

In Jesus' first battle with the enemy, at the very beginning of his public ministry, we're told that three times the devil came to tempt him in the desert (Matthew 4:1–11). And three times he was ready. Alert. Armed with the truth of God's Word. With eyes wide open, he was ready for the fight.

No wonder, then, toward the end of his public ministry, he gave that simple yet profound command to "watch and pray." It's no wonder that years later, Peter would write: "Be alert and of sober mind. Your enemy the devil prowls around like a roaring lion looking for someone to devour" (1 Peter 5:8). He knew all too well what it was like *not* to be ready, watchful, and alert.

So where is Jesus calling you to keep your eyes open? Is it in your marriage? Your family? At school or work? Where is the enemy trying to discourage you and disrupt the good work God is doing in you and through you? Be watchful, friend. Keep your eyes open and fixed on Jesus. He is with you and fighting for you!

POINTS TO PONDER

Where are you most tempted right now?

_____

Jesus calls us to be alert. To be watchful and pray. We should not walk in fear, but we should walk in wisdom. List a few ways you can be more awake to this battle around you.

_____

_____

PAUSING TO PRAY

Jesus, I know you are with me and fighting for me. Help me to be watchful with _____

_____

12 | I Am Here for You

Karen

Scripture to Study

I know that I will remain and continue with all of you for your progress and joy in the faith.

Philippians 1:25 CSB

My three children shared a bedroom when they were young, sleeping in a triple bunk bed. Ballet tights and Batman pj's happily resided side-by-side in their dresser. Then, one day we moved to a new house, giving our daughter her own bedroom separate from the boys.

Our two-year-old had a difficult time adjusting to sleeping without his big sister in the room. To alleviate his distress, my daughter would pray with him that God would enable him to settle down, and then she'd lie on his floor until he fell asleep. Just knowing she was nearby was enough to alleviate his fears, allowing his anxious mind to calm and his fidgety body to finally drift off to sleep.

In the letter of Philippians, the apostle Paul discusses longing to be in heaven with Christ but also desiring to remain here on earth near his friends to strengthen and encourage them (Philippians 1:20–26). Then he states, "I know that I will remain and continue with all of you for your progress and joy in the faith."

There is a wordplay in the original language of this verse that isn't easily reproduced in English. When the apostle says he will both *remain* and *continue*, the Greek words *menein* and *paramenein* were initially used. The word *menein* means to remain with, or to continually be in close proximity, referring to a person's physical location. However, the word *paramenein* hitches a prefix, adding a new dimension. This term means to linger physically beside a person, ever ready to help.

It is as if Paul is relaying two crucial truths to his friends: "I'm here" and "I'm here for you." How this letter must have encouraged their hearts, enabling their anxious minds to rest by knowing their father in the faith was in close proximity, ready to assist them if needed.

Later, in Philippians 4:5, Paul writes, "Let your graciousness be known to everyone. The Lord is near" (CSB). The Greek term for *near* here meant both near in time and near in proximity. The apostle may have been referring to the Lord's future earthly return. However, the word also carries the thought of God being close in proximity, ready to come to their aid.

The ministry of proximity means that we, as believers, stand nearby each other, ready to help when necessary. However, this concept is most prominently displayed by the Lord himself toward us. Even when we don't sense it, our heavenly Father is near, ready to comfort, calm, and console. He alone is our ever-present help in times of trouble (Psalm 46:1).

POINTS TO PONDER

How do you find your heart encouraged when you think of the Lord saying both "I am here" and also "I am here for you"?

_____

Paul desired to see the Philippian church members make progress in their faith and obtain joy. Today, we can use our words and our presence to help others grow and bring them joy. Write down the name of one fellow believer whom you will encourage and cheer this week.

_____

PAUSING TO PRAY

Father, at those times I can't sense you near, help me to remember

_____

_____

13 | How Not to Get Lost

Ruth

Scripture to Study

When Pharaoh let the people go, God did not lead them on the road through the Philistine country, though that was shorter.

Exodus 13:17

When was the last time you got lost? Or at least felt lost? I remember as a child walking through a packed fairground, looking up to see my parents were no longer by me. It was so crowded, and I was alone. Disoriented. And terrified that I would not find my way back to my parents!

There is a story early on in the Bible, the story of God's people, the Israelites, finally being let go out of their slavery in Egypt. Plague after plague would not loosen the grip Pharaoh had on the Hebrews, but ultimately, the hardness of Pharaoh's heart met the hand of God in dramatic fashion and he let them go.

Being *let go* is one thing. Learning to *hold on* is quite another. One sets you free; the other keeps you from getting lost on the journey!

In Exodus 13:17, we're told that "when Pharaoh let the people go, God did not lead them on the road through the Philistine country, though that was shorter." Did you catch that? "God did not lead them on the road" that would have been "shorter." In other words, God was taking his people on a different route. He had a better plan. A wiser path. But in order *not* to get lost, they would have to *hold on*. They would have to trust God's wisdom and direction.

The more predictable path and shorter route would have been along the ancient and well-traveled highway that ran along the sea. But anticipating that route to be more dangerous for his people at that time,

God took them along a different route. A longer path. One that would eventually fool the Egyptians into following the Israelites to the Red Sea. God's people would indeed be let go as the sea swallowed the Egyptians.

If you read the next several chapters in Exodus, you discover the greater challenge will be getting Egypt out of God's people! They'll have to learn to walk with God, trust him, and stay close to him.

Are you in a season or set of circumstances that has you feeling lost or disoriented? My prayer for you is that God would give you the courage to walk the path he has chosen for you. May he give you the grace to not only accept it but to embrace it. And as you hold on to him, may your heart be aligned with his. It is God's choice to lead, but ours to follow.

POINTS TO PONDER

Has God led you somewhere that is hard to understand?

I'm reminded from these verses that God knows best. He knows what we need, when we need it, and where we need it. If God has led you down a path that seems different or confusing, write down a few ways you can intentionally remember God's wisdom, faithfulness, and presence on the journey.

_____

_____

_____

_____

PAUSING TO PRAY

Father, you know what is best, and so I will trust you with _____

_____

14 | A Peace That's Out of This World

Karen

Scripture to Study

I am leaving you with a gift—peace of mind and heart. And the peace I give is a gift the world cannot give. So don't be troubled or afraid.

John 14:27 NLT

I plopped myself on the living room couch and grabbed the remote to zone out for a while. After a stressful day of Zoom meetings and work responsibilities—and not nearly enough time to tend to anything around the house—my mind was restless, and my heart lacked peace. I was hoping that numbing my brain by watching a show would help me to relax awhile and rejuvenate.

As I flipped through the channels, I spied a commercial that promised to usher in peace with a trip to a new local salon. Maybe that was what I needed! Having some downtime to grab a relaxing massage or have my toenails painted a pretty shade of pale peach might be the remedy to what ailed me.

A little while later, yet another digital advertisement suggested that serenity could be achieved by hopping online and clicking for tickets to a tropical getaway, complete with gourmet food and breathtaking views of the ocean. The imagery looked so tranquil that—if I could have afforded it—I would have grabbed my phone and secured myself a spot smack-dab in the middle of that magnificent paradise.

But I know from experience that while a day at the salon or a trip designed for relaxation might give us a little breather, they are not what our hearts and minds most need.

In the book of John, Jesus promises us a wonderful gift: peace of mind and heart. This isn't accomplished by even the best package deal the world's salons or travel agencies have to offer. Christ declares, "The peace I give is a gift the world cannot give."

When we see the word *world*, we might think of the earth and the people and systems who reside there. However, the Greek word translated here as *world* has a nuanced meaning. It is referring to the affairs and adornments of the world.[1]

The world offers us activities. It attempts to dress and adorn to give us a better existence. Certainly, in some cases this helps. There are businesses and companies in the world that can help to dress us fashionably or adorn our homes with beautiful decor. But our hearts and minds are an altogether different story. Outward embellishments and activities don't produce lasting peace.

The peace Jesus promises literally means having a heart and mind that are undisturbed and whole. That are no longer disquieted. That can rest assured and not be afraid, knowing God is in control. This is a peace that surpasses all human understanding (Philippians 4:7).

Is your heart unsettled or your mind uneasy? Take your troubles to Jesus. He sees. He hears and he also listens. He alone can provide serenity for your soul.

POINTS TO PONDER

Where are some of the places you have tried to find serenity?

_____

_____

_____

_____

_____

_____

What one action step will you take this week that will position you to seek the peace that only Jesus can offer?

_____

_____

_____

PAUSING TO PRAY

Heavenly Father, *forgive me for looking for peace anywhere other than from you. Empower me to* _____

_____

_____

_____

15 | Give Me the Right Feet

Ruth

Scripture to Study

The Sovereign LORD is my strength;
   he makes my feet like the feet of a deer,
   he enables me to tread on the heights.

Habakkuk 3:19

Incurable.

That is the word that lifted off my computer screen as I sat on our bed, not long after we heard the C word. There was no getting around this. The cancer my husband had just been diagnosed with was going to be a fight.

I could feel the strength being sucked out of me like water that quickly evaporates in the heat of a summer day. I was gasping for air and gasping for answers. How could this be happening to *us*? I had no idea how we were going to get through this. There are some things we walk through in life. And then there are things we walk *with* for the rest of our life. This was something God was going to have to give us the grace to get through.

Since that day, my husband and I have talked often about a picture he took in Israel years ago. It is a shot of mountain goats, or ibex, that climb up the steep slopes in a region called Ein Gedi. Ein Gedi is just to the west and north of the Dead Sea. It is like an oasis in the dry and dusty wilderness. It is also where most scholars believe David hid in a cave when being pursued by King Saul. It also happens to be a favorite, though seemingly dangerous, place for these mountain goats or deer to roam.

And they did so with such ease. Their path was so dangerous, but their feet seemed steady. There are several places in Scripture that mention these mountain deer, but this is one of our favorites:

> The Sovereign LORD is my strength;
>> he makes my feet like the feet of a deer,
>> he enables me to tread on the heights.
>
> Habakkuk 3:19

One of our favorite Bible teachers, Ray Vander Laan, helped us see this point. It's not the path that makes the journey walkable—it's the feet. It is the Lord who strengthens us on any path. He gives us the right feet to keep walking, one foot after another after another!

What do the right feet look like? I think they are feet that are walking in obedience to God's Word (Psalm 119:105). They are feet that are walking in wisdom (Proverbs 3:23). They are feet aimed in the direction of Jesus, the Light of the World (John 10:11). So will you pray for the path today or the right feet? Remember, the Lord strengthens you and makes your feet like the "feet of deer," enabling you to "tread on the heights."

POINTS TO PONDER

What difficult path are you walking right now?

_____

_____

_____

_____

_____

_____

_____

We rarely get to choose our path. Sometimes we find ourselves in a season or set of circumstances that feels dangerous or impossible to walk through. By God's grace, he gives us the right feet no matter the path. How will the way you walk look different with this in mind?

_____

_____

_____

_____

_____

PAUSING TO PRAY

Father, *give me the right feet to* _____

_____

_____

_____

_____

16 | When Your Mouth Needs a Recall Button

Karen

Scripture to Study

A good man brings good things out of the good stored up in his heart, and an evil man brings evil things out of the evil stored up in his heart. For the mouth speaks what the heart is full of.

Luke 6:45

Have you ever thought about the myriad ways technology allows us to talk to each other? We can do video calls on our cell phones or hop on our computers and hold online meetings, and our phones even allow us to talk while we're in a remote location or traveling far away.

One of my favorite ways to talk to my friends is by using a phone app that acts much like an old-fashioned walkie-talkie. It enables you to speak in real time to someone else who has the app. Or, if you happen to be busy at the time, the app holds the message from the sender until you have time to open it and listen.

This app also has a recall feature: If you leave a message for someone but change your mind about their hearing it, you can recall (or delete) the message, or you can leave a different, better message instead. Now, if only I had a recall button for my actual life!

I think back to the many times I've regretted my words. Maybe I spoke something in haste or I was careless in my word choice and sent an inaccurate message. Usually I spoke in anger or frustration and, as a result, regretted my words. Honestly, the root of the problem isn't in the speaking. It is in the storing.

Luke 6:45 states, "The mouth speaks what the heart is full of." The loose translation? You are going to speak what you have stored. If you store resentment toward someone, it may come tumbling out one day in angry words. If you store bitterness about a past hurt, you might find yourself suddenly spilling caustic criticism. If you store unforgiveness in your heart, it may bubble to the surface and show up in unkind speech.

You are going to speak what you have stored.

To reduce the chances of spilling out unsweet speech, we need to continually ask God to reveal any destructive feelings lurking in the dark corners of our hearts. Surrendering these corrosive and unhealthy feelings to him can prevent us from spilling out words we later regret. Preaching this little, one-sentence sermon to ourselves can also help: *Don't say something permanently painful just because you're temporarily ticked off.*

When we make it both our prayer and our aim to speak words that are kind, we have less need for a recall button for our mouths. Instead, we'll find ourselves sprinkling sweet speech around us, improving our relationships, and preventing a boatload of regret.

POINTS TO PONDER

Is there a time in the past when you wished you had a recall button for your mouth? How can you handle similar situations differently today?

_____

_____

_____

PAUSING TO PRAY

Father, help me store up that which is good in my heart and keep me from _____

_____

17 | When Words Are Hard to Find

Ruth

Sometimes it is hard to pray. At times, it feels impossible to wrap words around deep wounds or longings of the heart. We sit and weep. Rock back and forth. Toss and turn. Or maybe we grasp for a word, like a child on a summer night trying to catch a firefly. Just when we think we have caught it, we open our hand, only to find it empty.

And so, in these moments or seasons, spontaneous prayers are hard to pray. It's like we need someone else to pray for us! Here is the good news if you are in that place, my friend. We stand in a long line of faithful followers of Jesus who have experienced every joy and every sorrow we encounter. We have so many prayers from lovers of God who came before us.

The church has a long history of praying these *vocal prayers*. These are prayers written by someone else. Such cries of the heart, like the psalms, help us move slowly through every range of human emotion. They guide us, giving us words when none can be found. And ultimately, they give us words that, like windows, open our heart to the love and truth of God. Prayer pries our hearts open for the presence of God to heal us.

One of my favorite examples of this kind of prayer, which the church has prayed since Jesus first taught it, is the Lord's Prayer.

This, then, is how you should pray:

"Our Father in heaven,
hallowed be your name,

56

your kingdom come,
your will be done,
    on earth as it is in heaven.
Give us today our daily bread.
And forgive us our debts,
    as we also have forgiven our debtors.
And lead us not into temptation,
    but deliver us from the evil one."

Matthew 6:9–13

Maybe you grew up in a tradition that prayed this prayer often. Early sources outside of the Bible tell us that many followers of Jesus prayed this prayer three times a day. But more than just praying this prayer as routine or ritual, pray this prayer meditating and expanding on each phrase.

Join me in this prayer today. Slowly. Open your heart and let the presence of God heal you, encourage you, and remind you of who he is—a Father in heaven who cares for you.

POINTS TO PONDER

How do written prayers, such as the psalms or the Lord's Prayer, help you know how to feel?

_____

_____

_____

_____

One of the gifts of prayer is that we can honestly come to the Lord as our good Father. But these written prayers not only express for us *what* we are feeling but also tell us *how* to feel, in light of who God is. As you begin to pray these prayers, pay attention to how prayer can "correct" how we feel in light of God's character and promises.

PAUSING TO PRAY

Our Father in heaven, hallowed be your name. . . .

_____

_____

_____

_____

_____

_____

_____

_____

_____

18 | Successful or Suffering?

Karen

Scripture to Study

Consider it a great joy, my brothers and sisters, whenever you experience various trials, because you know that the testing of your faith produces endurance. And let endurance have its full effect, so that you may be mature and complete, lacking nothing.

James 1:2–4 CSB

The whole current culture of social media has really changed the way we look at people. Years ago, someone was either a regular person or they had some degree of fame. But today there is a whole new category of people: those regular people who garner a level of fame because of a video gone viral or a social media account they set up with the goal of becoming an "influencer." This is a person who is able to generate interest in something (such as a consumer product) by posting about it on social media.

Even in the Christian realm, we find such influencers who are wildly popular. People long to connect with them, even going so far as to send them a private message. There is just something about us that wants to rub shoulders with a Christian we think is successful.

But a friend of mine once made a statement I'll never forget. She said that when faced with a choice between spending time with a successful Christian or a suffering one, you should choose the suffering one every time.

In the book of James, we are told to consider trials a great joy because the testing of our faith will produce endurance. In the original Greek language, the word translated as "trials" in James 1:2 meant a testing, temptation, calamity, or affliction.[1] As awful as those situations sound, we are told that once we've waded through these trying times, it will produce in us endurance. The endurance described here portrays a steadfast patience that is willing to remain behind. Such endurance has an outcome: We become mature and complete, lacking nothing.

We grow in maturity when we bear up under our trials, developing perseverance. It is interesting that we are encouraged to "allow endurance to have its full effect." This suggests that we might short-circuit the result when we try to wiggle out of the trials we are facing. However, when we are willing to stand firm, facing the trials and relying on God in the process, our faith becomes mature and complete.

I have known several suffering Christians who remained steadfast and withstood during dreadful trials in their life. Some trials were relational. Others were physical or financial. And still others were medical in nature. All these suffering saints had a distinctive and deep spiritual maturity. And my friend was right—I would much rather spend time with them, soaking in the wisdom and perspective they had gained from the Lord, than with any famous Christian influencer out there!

May we not shy away from our suffering, knowing God is at work growing our faith and making us spiritually mature. This maturity can encourage others to also persevere as they face their own unique trials, spurring them on in their spiritual development.

POINTS TO PONDER

Can you name a Christian who has endured a great trial in their life? What did you notice about their faith that seemed spiritually mature?

_____

_____

PAUSING TO PRAY

Father, forgive me for the times I've wished for social notoriety rather than spiritual maturity. Help me in the future to _____

_____

19 | Rest for the Restless

Ruth

Scripture to Study

Come to me, all you who are weary and burdened, and I will give you rest.

Matthew 11:28

Jesus is not the only one who says, "Come to me," is he? We are constantly being bombarded with other invites, different offers. Visions, if you will, of what we think will make us happy. Or put us at rest.

We can get stuck in the scroll on social media and, before we know it, we are following everyone else's amazing life! For all the promises that social media offers, rarely do I feel full. I usually feel weary and burdened.

We always want more. We're always looking and longing for better. Or different. We get hooked by comparison, the desire for more money, travel, the promise of pleasure, status, or success. It's like we are drinking from little puddles that quickly dry up, as we dart back and forth in front of the source of Living Water. Yet there Jesus is, patiently and lovingly waiting. He calls to us. "I have what you are looking for."

In Matthew 11:28, we read Jesus' invitation. Once again, we see his pursuit of us. His gracious call to lay down all that is dead and dying in our lives. Everything that has us distracted and worn out. "Rest is right in front of you," Jesus is saying. The promise is that he takes our weary, burdened, and thirsty souls and fills them up with himself. He reveals how empty we really are apart from him. We can't live long or well disconnected from the source of all that is good. "Come to me . . . and I will give you rest."

So what has you worn out? Is there something that has you burdened? Maybe today is the day to get free. Find true and lasting rest by simply spending time with Jesus. Here is the simple promise, my friend: Jesus will give you rest. He will put your troubled heart at ease. Jesus not only settles our soul; Jesus satisfies our soul. And the promise is available to us today.

POINTS TO PONDER

Who or what are you following that has you worn out?

_____

_____

_____

Rest is not always about getting away or finding some peace and quiet. Ultimately, rest is found in walking with Jesus. But in order to follow Jesus more, we need to follow others less. Spend some time in prayer, asking the Lord to show you who or what you are following that is wearing you out.

PAUSING TO PRAY

Jesus, *give me the courage to say yes to you and to say no to following* _____

_____

_____

_____

20 | When Your Prison Becomes Your Platform

Karen

Scripture to Study

I want you to know, brothers, that what has happened to me has really served to advance the gospel.

Philippians 1:12 ESV

One spring day, I took my three young children to a historic village that included a jailhouse from the late 1800s. I snapped a playful picture of them peering out from behind the bars of that prison cell, grinning wide for the camera. In reality, however, prisons are certainly nothing to smile about.

Paul wrote the letter of Philippians while a prisoner, most likely in the city of Rome around the year AD 62. This was about a decade after the founding of the church at Philippi. He'd been abandoned by many of his friends (2 Timothy 4:9–18). Others—even fellow believers—had spoken out against him, hoping to get him into trouble with the government, and many Bible scholars believe he might possibly have been facing execution for his faith.

Notice the way Paul rotates the narrative and reframes his incarceration. He doesn't complain about his physical location. Instead, he rejoices in the progress being made in the eternal realm. What was meant to handcuff him physically was not able to shackle him spiritually. His prison became a platform from which he could spread the good news about Jesus.

Those nearest in physical proximity to Paul—the imperial guard—heard the gospel. Sometimes referred to as the Praetorian Guard, these men were a select group of personal bodyguards who protected the Roman emperor. The news of the gospel of Jesus didn't stop there. A multiplying effect occurred, ensuring even more people heard the salvation story. (These happenings are seen in Philippians 1:13–14.)

When Paul's story was told, it included the why—Jesus. The unusual reason for Paul's incarceration was not for any real crime, but for his faith. Naturally, others would be curious. If this man hadn't broken any laws, why was he behind bars?

Finally, others were emboldened when they saw Paul use his chains as an invitation to preach. His Philippian friends weren't reading a letter from a bewildered and panicked person questioning, "What has happened to me?" Those same words became a calm and insightful statement instead: "What has happened to me has really served to advance the gospel."

Many of us find ourselves in situations that feel confining. We might feel stuck in a job, in a hard relationship, or even with a physical challenge or illness that limits us. Let Paul's example spark your own faith, prompting you to cry out to God. Not, "Lord, please get me out of here!" But rather, "Father, why have you brought me here?"

The answer is the same one given to Paul: so that others will see and hear the gospel through you and will also learn to place their trust in the Lord.

POINTS TO PONDER

Though Paul's chains were intended to impede him, he chose to see them as an occasion to share about Jesus. Is there something in your life that threatens to place you in an emotional prison?

How can you utilize this situation to present the gospel with others?

_____

_____

_____

PAUSING TO PRAY

Father God, *please grant me an eternal perspective, one that sees my current predicament as a platform to* _____

_____

_____

_____

_____

_____

---

21 | I Can't (and Don't Have to) Do It All

Ruth

Scripture to Study

Blessed are the poor in spirit, for theirs is the kingdom of heaven.

Matthew 5:3

Trusting God in all the things means trusting God with the many circumstances in life that include the things we can't do. And many things maybe we shouldn't be doing. There is rest in knowing it's not all up to us!

When Jesus went up on the mountainside to teach what it looks like to live with God as King in our lives, he began with the simple and yet profound truth that it is the "poor in spirit" who inherit the "kingdom of heaven."

It's not the proud. Or the powerful. It's not the ones who have it all together. It's the ones who see their sins and have no solution in themselves.

"Blessed are the poor in spirit, for theirs is the kingdom of heaven," Jesus says in Matthew 5:3. The happy life, Jesus is telling us, is when we come to the end of ourselves. We recognize we are powerless to save ourselves. We have no remedy for our sin other than Jesus. It is the grace of God, his underserving love and forgiveness, that sets us free and settles our soul. Through repentance and faith, we come to Jesus poor yet become rich.

To be poor in spirit is to know and live out of our powerlessness—first and foremost in our relationship with God, but also in our relationship with others. It is to have our heart settled, knowing that all does not depend on us!

To be poor in spirit is necessary for our salvation with God, and often times it is necessary to maintain our sanity with others!

It is to say . . .

I can't do everything on my own.

I can't say yes to everyone.

I can't solve every problem.

Everyone's crisis is not my responsibility.

I can pray for you.

I can love you, but not fix you.

I am poor in spirit, but I know the One who is rich in wisdom, power, and goodness.

Friend, if you are feeling worn out and burdened, there is rest and freedom available to you. The invitation Jesus is offering you is to come to him. Admit your poverty, be okay with your powerlessness, and let him be God! Both in your relationship with him *and* in your relationship with others.

POINTS TO PONDER

How can admitting your "poverty" benefit you most right now?

_____

_____

_____

Trusting God in all the things means trusting God with all the things we can't or shouldn't be doing. How can setting healthy boundaries actually improve your relationships?

_____

_____

_____

_____

PAUSING TO PRAY

Father, *I can't do it all. I know I am poor in spirit. And so I am releasing* _____

_____

_____

_____

_____

_____

22 | Following from Close Behind

Karen

Scripture to Study

I follow close to you; your right hand holds on to me.

Psalm 63:8 CSB

When it comes to purchasing books, I much prefer a mom-and-pop brick-and-mortar bookstore over an online source. Besides the fact that I like to shop local, there is just something about walking in and perusing the volumes standing at attention on the shelves. I adore holding them in my hands and flipping through the pages. And, if the bookstore also boasts a quaint café with a delicious vanilla bean latte, then I might just spend an entire afternoon shopping for a new title or two.

A few weeks ago, however, I needed to purchase a book online because I was having it shipped to a friend's house. I'd seen her posting online how much she's always wanted one of those journaling Bibles, designed with the wide margins for either drawing illustrations or jotting down notes. So as a little "unbirthday" present, I logged on and had one sent to her house.

Once my on-screen checkout was complete, a pop-up window appeared before my eyes. I have seen this pop-up many times when ordering a book. But this instance made me chuckle. It tossed out a question that read, "Would you like to follow the author?" Apparently, the auto response that came with a purchase couldn't differentiate between a human author and the Author of life itself.

In Psalm 63:8 the psalmist declares, "I follow close to you; your right hand holds on to me." Just what does it mean to truly follow God?

The Hebrew word for follow, *dabaq*, means to cling to, cleave, or hold fast to.[1] It is a method of following so closely that you are almost stuck to the person or object. The original words in this phrase also give a deeper shade of meaning to our English phrase *close to you*. The single Hebrew word *achar* is used, which denotes afterward, from the rear, or pursuing from close behind.[2]

If we truly want to follow the Author of life, might we more effectively do this if we remembered that it's not we who should set the agenda and then ask God to bless our plans? Rather, we should be properly positioned behind him, pursuing him closely in our thoughts and actions. I know I too often get ahead of God rather than trustingly follow him from behind. This verse in Psalms is a simple reminder that I am not in the lead. I need to follow behind the Lord—and not from afar. I want to cling to, cleave to, and hold fast to his Word, allowing him to lead the way. Any other such arrangement is only a recipe for disaster.

Will you commit to following the Author of the Bible today, allowing him to lead and clinging to his Word—the very Word of life? (Philippians 2:15–17). He knows the way you should go, and he won't ever lead you astray.

POINTS TO PONDER

In your current walk with God, which statement below most closely describes you? Circle the one that best applies.

- I have been following closely behind him.
- I've been trying furiously to play a game of catch-up.
- I've been trying to lead the way, hoping he would bless my plans.

How can the explanation of what it means to follow God closely help you rearrange your thinking and alter your actions going forward?

_____

_____

_____

PAUSING TO PRAY

Father God, *I long to follow you closely. I commit to* _____

_____

_____

_____

_____

_____

23 | Repairing Broken Relationships

Ruth

Scripture to Study

First go and be reconciled to them; then come and offer your gift.

Matthew 5:24

When a relationship is suffering, we typically have one of two responses: We try to repair it or we try to repay it. Recently, in the middle of a podcast that my husband and I host, I made a confession to him. Ironically, we had just had a misunderstanding the day before and we were doing an episode on forgiveness, so it felt like the perfect time to apologize. Ha!

We were talking about how we all sin against others and others sin against us. As sinners relating to other sinners, we find that conflict, disappointment, misunderstanding, and offense are inevitable. Without the gift of forgiveness, no relationships stand a chance of making it. And this is the point at which I told my husband that the way I usually deal with hurt in a relationship is by withdrawing! Fortunately, our conflict with one another is fairly minimal.

Repairing broken relationships is no small thing to Jesus. Given that we have received this free gift of forgiveness by God through faith in Jesus, it follows that we should be a gracious people. We are routinely commanded to forgive because we have been forgiven. Our willingness to forgive is proof we have experienced the life-changing forgiveness made available to us through the death and resurrection of Jesus.

But the truth is, reconciling relationships can be hard. It can take time and healing—and lots of God's grace to enable us to move toward someone who has hurt us instead of away from them. This is the point of Jesus' teaching in Matthew 5.

> Therefore, if you are offering your gift at the altar and there remember that your brother or sister has something against you, leave your gift there in front of the altar. First go and be reconciled to them; then come and offer your gift.
>
> (vv. 23–24)

Notice that Jesus says if you remember that a "brother or sister has something against you," not, "if you have something against them." We are to wait. Repair the broken relationship first.

If that's not enough, Jesus is teaching this passage in Galilee. So when he says leave your "gift at the altar," he is likely referring to a sacrifice being left at the altar in the temple, which was not in Galilee but in Jerusalem. So if a Galilean is hearing Jesus say this, he is thinking, *I have to walk all the way to Jerusalem first to make the offering, then leave it there while I walk back to Galilee to right the wrong, and then travel all the way back to Jerusalem to worship?* Yes, Jesus says! In God's eyes, there is that kind of urgency to repair, not repay, broken relationships.

So who is it Jesus is calling you to move toward in humility and grace? Don't wait. Make the first move. No matter how far you have to go.

POINTS TO PONDER

How are you tempted to repay a broken relationship?

_____

Forgiveness is never something we do in our strength. Write down the name of a friend with whom you know you need to reconcile. Ask God to give you his grace to do what is right and work toward repairing your hurting friendship.

_____

PAUSING TO PRAY

Father, give me the grace to be reconciled to my friend. Help me to take the first step today by _____

73

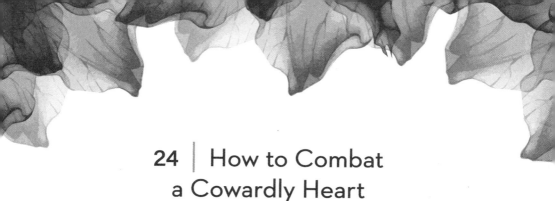

24 | How to Combat a Cowardly Heart

Karen

Scripture to Study

Say to the cowardly: "Be strong; do not fear! Here is your God; vengeance is coming. God's retribution is coming; he will save you."

Isaiah 35:4 CSB

My mom, brother, and I whipped up a buttery batch of popcorn using our noisy—but trusty—air-pop machine. We then settled ourselves on the sofa in our living room where we were about to watch one of my favorite childhood movies on network television: *The Wizard of Oz.*

What a myriad of memorable characters there are in this classic. I wanted to wear my hair in two ponytails just like the main character, Dorothy, and my wardrobe would be complete if I could just own a pair of sparkly ruby slippers. I always felt sorry for the Tin Man, I was terrified of the flying monkeys, and I didn't want to get anywhere near their boss—the Wicked Witch of the West. But the creature I was most endeared by was the Cowardly Lion.

Afraid of his own shadow, this not-so-ferocious feline wanted only one thing in life: courage. And he thought he could receive it from the great and powerful Oz.

There are times in real life when I find myself quite cowardly. I'm afraid of taking a risk. Or I am fearful that one of my family members might make a bad or immoral choice. I have financial uncertainties at times. And most recently, I have a dread of terminal medical diagnoses, since losing five family members to incurable illnesses in the last two years.

Thankfully, we don't place our hopes for being granted courage in a mythical creature ultimately revealed to be a mere human. We have access to the great and powerful God of the universe. Hear his words written in the book of Isaiah:

> Be strong; do not fear! Here is your God; vengeance is coming. God's retribution is coming; he will save you.

Oh, how I love that these directives are pointedly addressed to "the cowardly"! In the original Hebrew language, this phrase points to the inner man, will, or mind in contrast to the outer man, whose emotions and fears show. That means that this fearful heart—literally a heart full of fear—is something no one else even sees.

Do you harbor hidden fears in your heart? Are there things you are dreading that no one else knows about but Jesus? Do you keep a stiff upper lip and maintain a stance of courage when all the while your mind is racing, worrying about something you dread may come to pass?

We can find strength and a calm resolve in the words of this verse. "Be strong; do not fear!" And *how* can we be strong and face our fears? The answer comes in the very next phrase: "Here is your God!" He is ever beside us, ready to infuse us with courage.

Only God can take a cowardly heart and transform it into one of bravery and boldness. When your heart begins to fear, remind it of this: "Here is your God!" We need not be frightened any longer.

POINTS TO PONDER

What hidden fear do you have in your heart that perhaps no one else knows about?

_____

_____

_____

How can the words of Isaiah 35:4 infuse your fearful heart with courage? Which words or phrases mean the most to you?

_____

_____

_____

_____

_____

──── **PAUSING TO PRAY** ────────────────

Father, *when I sense some cowardice creeping into my heart, help me to* _____

_____

_____

_____

25 | Heavy Crosses

Ruth

Scripture to Study

As the soldiers led him away, they seized Simon from Cyrene, who was on his way in from the country, and put the cross on him and made him carry it behind Jesus.

Luke 23:26

What has caught you by surprise lately? Is there something that has entered your life unexpectedly? The story of Simon the Cyrene is a story of surprises. It's an event, or set of circumstances, that he could not have predicted, nor would he have wanted. But it would also be transformative and life-altering.

We don't know a lot about Simon, other than that he was likely visiting the city of Jerusalem for the feast of Passover. We do know there was much that had already happened in the recent events of Jesus' life.

He was betrayed by some of his closest friends.

Alone with his Father, he was stretched to the limits of human suffering in the Garden of Gethsemane.

He was arrested.

Questioned by Pilate and Herod.

Tortured and mocked.

Told to carry his cross to the place of skulls.

But here is where Simon meets Jesus—on the way to his crucifixion. Under the heavy burden of the cross. The weight was so enormous physically, emotionally, and spiritually, that it is a Roman soldier who calls Simon out of the crowds to carry the cross for Jesus and with Jesus. A surprise to be sure. But the intrusion would also be an instrument. The cross, when embraced, is always an instrument to conform us into the likeness of Jesus.

Notice that Luke tells us Simon carried the cross of Jesus "behind" Jesus. Earlier in Luke's gospel, he reminds us of the way of Jesus: "Whoever wants to be my disciple must deny themselves and take up their cross daily and follow me. For whoever wants to save their life will lose it, but whoever loses their life for me will save it" (Luke 9:23–24).

Simon was confronted with a cross he didn't ask for. But he chose to carry it behind Jesus and with Jesus anyway. There are some crosses we choose. But it seems the ones we are asked to carry by surprise can also be the ones that draw us closer to and make us more like Jesus in the end.

POINTS TO PONDER

What crosses have caught you by surprise?

_____

Discipleship is never easy. The trials we face can feel like intrusions. But in God's hands, they can also be instruments of growth and transformation. How is God asking you to draw closer to him through these trials today?

_____

_____

_____

PAUSING TO PRAY

Father, _give me the strength to carry the cross of_ _____

_____

26 | Reach for the Living Water

Karen

Scripture to Study

The person who trusts in the LORD,
whose confidence indeed is the LORD, is blessed.

He will be like a tree planted by water:
it sends its roots out toward a stream,
it doesn't fear when heat comes,
and its foliage remains green.
It will not worry in a year of drought
or cease producing fruit.

Jeremiah 17:7–8 CSB

When my husband and I purchased our first home, we knew there would inevitably be unexpected home repairs and maintenance issues we'd need to pay for along the way. The first one was a garbage disposal that stopped working suddenly, right as we were cleaning up the kitchen from having company over for dinner. Then, during our first cold Michigan January, our antiquated oil-burning furnace went on the blink. But perhaps the messiest and most entangled home debacle came when we found out the water pipes from our home to the city street had become completely plugged up.

Since we'd never owned a home before, we couldn't figure out what the issue might be. The repairman who came to our rescue discovered the problem. The thirty-year-old clay pipes had become entangled with knots and gnarls of massive tree roots.

This mystified me since there weren't any trees near where the backhoe had dug in our front yard. It was then that I learned a little lesson about trees. "Oh, ma'am," said the repairman. "A tree root's job is to search for water. They grow toward wherever they find moisture. So over the past thirty years, your trees have been stretching and reaching toward these pipes. Many of them found cracks in the pipes and just weaseled their way in. That's why you have such blockage."

We observe this exact concept in our passage of Scripture from Jeremiah today. A tree "sends its roots out toward a stream, it doesn't fear when heat comes, and its foliage remains green. It will not worry in a year of drought or cease producing fruit." And we, who want to be people who are trusting God in all the things, who place their confidence in him, should do the same.

Jesus Christ is the Living Water (John 4:10). If we are intentional to drink deep from the wealth of his Word, our roots will grow deep, we will not fear the heat of life, and like lush green foliage, we will grow and even produce fruit.

This won't always be stress-free. Like the wandering roots, you may need to stretch and strain in order to drink from the well. But God is faithful. He stands ever waiting, ready to fill us up so we can pour out.

May your roots go deep and may the Living Water quench your thirsty soul.

POINTS TO PONDER

Would you say you have been putting down roots deep in the Living Well, or is your spiritual life somewhat dry because you have neglected this endeavor?

What would you like to see change in this area?

PAUSING TO PRAY

Father, *you alone have the water that can quench my thirsty soul. In my walk with you I want to* _____

_____

_____

_____

_____

_____

_____

27 | Loving Others Freely

Ruth

Scripture to Study

When Paul had finished speaking, he knelt down with all of them and prayed. They all wept as they embraced him and kissed him. What grieved them most was his statement that they would never see his face again. Then they accompanied him to the ship.

Acts 20:36–38

Have you ever had to say good-bye to a dear friend? Someone you loved deeply?

My husband and I have been in local church ministry for over twenty years. It has been a privilege and a joy to share our lives with so many people along the way. As we have served in different churches and in different states, we have forged deep and meaningful relationships.

But we have also experienced the pain of learning to love people *freely*. As friends have moved and changed churches, or when we have been the ones to leave, we have felt the sting of good-byes and the sorrow of separation.

Acts 20 is one biblical illustration of just how hard those good-byes can be. The apostle Paul, before setting sail from Miletus, "sent to Ephesus for the elders of the church" (Acts 20:17). In the verses following, Paul shares the news of his departure, but also the gratitude in his heart for his faithful partners in ministry. Luke then tells us,

> When Paul had finished speaking, he knelt down with all of them and prayed. They all wept as they embraced him and kissed him. What grieved them most was his statement that they would never see his face again. Then they accompanied him to the ship.
>
> Acts 20:36–38

Good-byes are gut-wrenching, aren't they? Even if they aren't as dramatic or as permanent as Paul's good-bye. When, for whatever reason, we feel the sting of separation from a close friend, it is sobering.

But we need to remember that it is one thing to love a friend deeply but quite another to love them freely. Ultimately, our dearest of friends belong to God. We are to love them and open our hearts to be loved by them. When separation comes, we are to weep with them, pray for them, bless them, and ultimately surrender them to our Lord's loving care and purposes.

POINTS TO PONDER

What does it look like to love a friend freely?

_____

_____

Not only are we called to love deeply, but we are also called to love freely. We need to be grateful not only for the friends we have, but for how long we have them. And we need to always give thanks for how they love us, not for how we wish they would love us. What friend or friends do you need to love freely? Take a moment to pray for them.

_____

_____

_____

_____

PAUSING TO PRAY

Father, *teach me to love deeply. But also give me grace to love freely by* _____

_____

28 | Is There Enough?

Karen

Scripture to Study

But don't begin until you count the cost. For who would begin construction of a building without first calculating the cost to see if there is enough money to finish it?

Luke 14:28 NLT

About two years ago, we moved into a new house in a tiny quaint town smack-dab in the middle of the Mitten—Michigan. (Did you know we are America's high five?) We adored the charming brick exterior and colorful perennial landscaping. However, we knew the interior could use a little freshening up since most of it had not been touched for decades. So I spent my time parked in front of fixer-upper shows and nosing around on Pinterest, learning all about shiplap, subway tile, and neutral—but inviting—paint palettes.

Because we've never done simultaneous remodeling jobs before, I grew concerned I might go overboard when securing subcontractors and purchasing materials. So my husband and I crafted a budget and then made sure we put all the various bids together like puzzle pieces, ensuring that the total remodeling job would not break the bank.

The concept of budgeting doesn't just apply when you are resurfacing a fireplace or refinishing old hardwood floors. We also need to wisely budget our time. If we don't, we might find ourselves short on time but with a long list of activities that cause anxiety and can lead to chaos.

We read these cautionary words in Luke as they pertain to picking the construction of a building: *Don't begin until you count the cost*. Budgeting for building might seem like a no-brainer, but how many of us have launched into a new year, new semester, or even the summertime months without counting the cost of our time? Each of us only gets twenty-four hours a day. You do. I do. And twenty-four hours was all Jesus had each day.

The Lord had a busy life full of crowds to preach to, close friends to hang out with, and one-on-one encounters with souls who needed a touch from him. But he made sure that spending time alone with the Father was not crowded out of his schedule. He did not place tasks or other people above God.

If we have said yes to too many things, and now our commitments are crowding out time alone with God, we need to revisit our obligations and perhaps readjust. Let's wisely budget and then spend our time, making sure the important appointments are foremost on our schedules, especially the most important appointment with the Lord.

Have you calculated your time carefully and correctly, making sure to make time to connect with God?

POINTS TO PONDER

How do you rate when it comes to budgeting your time? Give yourself a number, with 1 being haphazard and 10 being extremely intentional.

How might you be more careful and prayerful so you are not stretched too thin?

_____

_____

_____

PAUSING TO PRAY

Father, *I want to carefully budget my time, making sure to allow plenty of space for connecting with you. This next week I want to*

_____

29 | Seeing Clearly

Ruth

Scripture to Study

Then God opened her eyes and she saw a well of water. So she went and filled the skin with water and gave the boy a drink.

Genesis 21:19

When has your suffering affected how you see? Distressing events have a way of distorting our vision, so we all need the reminder that even in the midst of our pain, God is our Provider. But we need his grace to see his goodness all around us.

In the Old Testament book of Genesis, we read the story of God's faithfulness to keep his Word and give Abraham and Sarah a child, even in their old age. In the opening verses of Genesis 21, we read, "Now the LORD was gracious to Sarah as he had said, and the LORD did for Sarah what he had promised. Sarah became pregnant and bore a son to Abraham in his old age, at the very time God had promised him. Abraham gave the name Isaac to the son Sarah bore him" (Genesis 21:1–3).

But if you remember the larger story, in the couple's waiting and disbelief, Hagar bore Abraham a son named Ishmael. Shortly after Isaac's birth, it was Sarah who asked Abraham to drive Hagar and her young son, Ishmael, away into the desert.

Deserts are distressing places. In the Bible, the desert is a place of testing and trial. It's not only dusty and dry, it's where things go to die. So it's no wonder Hagar, in her distress, begins to cry out to God. The water Abraham had given her was gone. The barrenness of the desert became a burden too great to carry.

But in her pain, here is where God begins to give her perspective. The writer of Genesis says it this way: "Then God opened her eyes and she saw a well of water. So she went and filled the skin with water and gave the boy a drink" (Genesis 21:19).

There, right in Hagar's midst, was the water she so desperately needed! She was just too overwhelmed to see it. It's easy to lose sight of God's provision in our pain. It might not be in the form of a well, but it could be in the form of a friend, a text at just the right moment, an email, a random act of kindness, or a hundred other "wells." Will you notice the drink God has provided for you? He always gives us enough water in our wandering.

POINTS TO PONDER

Where do you see God's provision in your distress?

_____

_____

_____

_____

_____

It's not always easy to see the goodness of God. So ask him to open your eyes as he did for Hagar. Pray that he might give you the grace you need to keep walking and trusting and loving.

PAUSING TO PRAY

Father, *thank you for the provision of* _____

_____

_____

30 | Give Him Your Best

Karen

On a sunny morning in June one year, I took my three small children to a local farmer's strawberry patch. He was finished picking for the season and gifted our family with the opportunity to pick the remaining strawberries to our hearts' content. My children were thrilled, and I was so looking forward to canning some strawberry banana jam to give as Christmas presents that year.

I parked baby Spencer in his car seat in a shady spot underneath a nearby maple tree where he took his morning nap. Toddler Mitchell wandered around eating more berries than he put in his bucket, the sticky crimson juice cascading down his beaming face. But our daughter, Kenna, was old enough to pick the berries without temptation, placing them meticulously in her bucket.

She seemed to be moving rather slowly through the berry patch, so I observed her to see what was taking her so long. She was painstakingly scrutinizing each berry before picking it off its branch and placing it in her bucket. I told her she didn't have to be so choosy; she only needed to make sure she wasn't picking berries that were still yellow or green. Her reply to me just melted my heart: "But, Mom, I want to give some strawberries to Daddy, so I have to find the very biggest and bestest ones!"

She wanted only to give her father the finest fruit she could offer.

Proverbs 3:9 urges us to honor the Lord with our wealth and to give him the best part of everything we produce. The first part of that proverb speaks of giving our money to the work of the Lord. But how about the second part? What does it mean to give the very best part of everything we produce to God?

To produce means to make, create, construct, or generate. Throughout our days we are producing. We make meals. We create atmospheres in our home. We forge friendships. We make time for quiet and create structure in our days. As we go about producing, do we strive to honor the Lord in these activities and relationships? Is our main objective, *How can what I am doing right now honor the Lord?* Or are we in such a hurry that we just forge ahead, checking items off our to-do list without ever really giving a thought to God? (Oh, am I preaching to myself on this one!)

Together, let's pledge that we will honor the Lord; that we'll attempt to give him the very best part of our day, of our thoughts, of our endeavors at creating and producing. He alone is worthy of our very "bestest" fruits and our utmost devotion.

POINTS TO PONDER

Would you say that honoring God is always at the forefront of your mind, even with mundane tasks, or do you tend to compartmentalize spiritual activities, separating them from tasks, chores, and responsibilities?

How can you be more intentional to give God your very best—even in the daily activities of life?

_____

_____

_____

PAUSING TO PRAY

Father, I want to give you the very best part of my heart and my days. This week, may I purpose to _____

31 | When God Feels Distant

Ruth

Scripture to Study

Let us then approach God's throne of grace with confidence, so that we may receive mercy and find grace to help us in our time of need.

Hebrews 4:16

"Where is God?" my friend asked, confiding in me. "I have been searching and seeking and I just don't feel his presence," she confessed. If we're honest, we've all had those seasons or circumstances when God seems far away. Times when we perceive him to be uninvolved or uninterested.

But the Scriptures remind us often that despite our feelings, God is not distant (Hebrews 13:5). He has not abandoned us. And while our feelings may come and go, the God of the Bible is a persistent, faithful, good, and present Friend on the journey.

One of the verses I have come back to over and over again in those seasons when God feels distant is Hebrews 4:16. The writer encourages us to come close to God. To close the gap. To consider that when we feel like God has moved, maybe we are the one who has moved. There is an invitation and a promise.

God is there. He is waiting for us to draw near to him. In a world with so many distractions, it is easy to go about our day or week or month and not think about God. We can become numb to the greatest reality there is—God himself. So what we need to do is reawaken to his presence—his abiding presence that has been there all along.

Because of what Jesus has accomplished for us on the cross, we have full access to God the Father in the power of the Holy Spirit. We can approach the throne of grace, not a throne of condemnation. We can come, covered in the blood of Jesus. With all of our hurts and questions and longings. When we do, we are met with grace. And in our time of need, whether it be great or small, we are showered with mercy and grace to help sustain us.

So if you feel like God is distant, draw near to him. He didn't move—you did. He is waiting for you today. Right now. He wants to give you his grace and mercy in your time of need.

POINTS TO PONDER

How can you draw close to God's abiding presence in your time of need?

_____

_____

_____

In seasons of dryness or distance, God is often teaching us to walk by faith and not by feeling. But he is also inviting us to draw near to him and be loved by him. We can never rush this. Where is God asking you to be patient today?

_____

_____

_____

PAUSING TO PRAY

Father, today I will draw near to your throne by _____

_____

_____

32 | Just Keep Moving

Karen

Scripture to Study

And let us not grow weary of doing good, for in due season we will reap, if we do not give up.

Galatians 6:9 ESV

Clip. *Clop.* Clip. *Clop.* The low murmur of bustling tourists was only eclipsed by the sound of dozens of horses' hooves as they pulled wagons of tourists through the quaint downtown city of Michigan's Mackinac Island.

This charming place in my home state is somewhat stuck in a time warp. There are no vehicles on the island; if you don't feel like walking, you can hail a taxicab that is pulled by one of the island's beautiful Belgian and Percheron draft horses.

While riding from our hotel room to the downtown area to sample some of the famous island fudge, our taxi driver told us some facts about the strong, beautiful horses that make life happen there. The horses keep pulling the carriages full of people—or the wagons full of packages for the post office or other parcel carrier—almost up until the time they die.

"Our horses don't retire," he explained. "If they do not keep working, they will quickly lose muscle mass, which greatly shortens their lifespan. If they want to live a long life, they have to just keep moving."

I've heard similar facts about other creatures in God's animal kingdom. There are certain varieties of sharks that must keep moving or else they will die. So they just keep swimming. (Right, Dory?)

In our spiritual lives, sometimes we don't want to keep moving ahead in certain relationships with others, those who are what I call prickly people—the rather hard-to-love sort. We get tired of treating them with kindness, behaving as God would have us to do, continuing to show up and show them love. We soon find ourselves worn out and weary.

Might we read Paul's words to the Galatian church as encouragement for us in such relationships today?

> And let us not grow weary of doing good, for in due season we will reap, if we do not give up.
>
> Galatians 6:9 ESV

The two Greek words used in this text that form our English phrase *doing good* have a combined meaning of being both honorable and commendable.[1] It is behavior that acts and also accomplishes. Our doing good both to and for others accomplishes something in God's kingdom. But this takes focus and patience.

The weariness described in this passage conveys the concept of being utterly spiritless, worn out, and even exhausted. I find I reach this state when I am doing good in my own strength or for my own purposes, such as when I am trying to please God or placate people. However, we don't do good deeds for good to be reciprocated. Nor do we view them as a way to earn God's eternal favor. We do kind deeds because God prepared in advance for us to do them (Ephesians 2:10).

Let's keep moving forward in our spiritual life, continuing to grow and live out our faith. To gather strength from God's work. To grab a renewed vision from time spent in prayer. Let us not give up and give in. There will come a harvest in due season, even if we never see it this side of heaven.

POINTS TO PONDER

Is there a situation where you have grown weary of doing good due to the behavior, or lack of response, from someone else? How might Galatians 6:9 encourage you not to give up but to keep forging ahead?

_____

_____

_____

PAUSING TO PRAY

Father, *I need your strength because I have grown weary from*

_____

_____

_____

_____

_____

_____

33 | We Need Less

Ruth

Scripture to Study

That you may be filled to the measure of all the fullness of God.

Ephesians 3:19

I fell into my familiar spot on the couch. The day was "over," or at least most of the day was over. The hard stuff was behind me. I had made it through another day of working from home, helping kids with school, dinner, and everything else that fills the gaps in between. I picked up my phone and immediately began to scroll. One picture after another. One post after another. Each image entering my eyes and etching its message on my heart. Before I knew it, I was hooked.

That would look good in our house.
I wonder why I didn't get invited to that girls' night?
I would love to go there someday, if only we could afford it!

Now, to be fair, what happened that particular night isn't always my experience, but it still happens too often. It is so easy for that sneaky and deceptive enemy of ours to get a foothold. One evening after the next of getting stuck in the scroll and, before I know it, I can believe that what I really need is more instead of less. More of what "they" have. Once again, I don't feel full. I feel empty. My soul isn't settled. My soul isn't satisfied. My soul feels starved.

So if you are anything like I am, then you need the reminder I need: *We likely need less in life, not more.* We need less information. Less comparison. Less stuff. And probably fewer things to do. What we need most, and what we do need more of, is what Paul prayed for in Ephesians 3—we need more of God.

I love how the apostle Paul comes to the middle of his letter to the church in Ephesus. For three and half chapters he's been writing about the mystery and goodness of God's love for us in Christ. And it's like he can't express it in any other way other than to simply pour out on paper his prayer for God's people.

What does he pray for us? He prays that instead of feeling empty and like we always need more, we might be "filled to the measure of all the fullness of God" (Ephesians 3:19).

Oh, how easy this can be to forget. I want to fill myself with the things of God, not the things of this world. When we allow ourselves to get sucked into social media and news and blogs and videos and all the things that show us all that we don't have but could have, we're missing out on all that God has for us right here and right now. He wants us to be satisfied in him. He wants us to want *less* of what the world offers and *all* of what he offers! To the fullness.

POINTS TO PONDER

Where do you struggle most right now with wanting more instead of less?

_____

We were created to know God, love him, and walk with him. The love of God in Christ is our deepest happiness, and yet our hearts can be restless. What are a few ways you can begin focusing less on what is passing and more on what is eternal today?

_____

_____

PAUSING TO PRAY

Father, give me a heart that is content. I confess that I often look for more by _____

34 | On Stashing and Storing

Karen

Scripture to Study

Your word I have treasured and stored in my heart,
That I may not sin against You.

Psalm 119:11 AMP

I closed my laptop in my home office and walked out to the kitchen to grab some more cold brew coffee from the fridge. It was a sunny 73-degree day, and I was contemplating perhaps taking my work out on the back deck to make some headway on my latest project out in the fresh springtime air.

As I rounded the corner into the kitchen, I spied my husband already out on the deck. He was putting the covers on the patio furniture, pulling the drawstrings tightly around the cushions. Then he cranked down the patio umbrella, securing it tightly with its Velcro fastener. "Hey. What are you doing?" I inquired through an open window. "I was just about to take my coffee out there and work."

"Check your weather app, Frances," he chirped back, tossing my middle name in for a tease. I tapped my way to a screen displaying the outlook for today's weather. Sure enough, it was 73 and sunny now with only a few puffy white clouds in sight. However, in less than a half hour, the brightly colored radar showed severe storms headed our way, bringing 90-degree temperatures and oppressive humidity along for the ride. A high wind advisory had also been issued, thus my husband's batten-down-the-hatches behavior. All cushions and pillows needed to be properly stashed away before the inclement weather arrived.

Just a few hours later, the meteorologists' predictions came true. Gusting winds, thunderbolts, and lightning flashed over our backyard. My husband's preparation had thwarted any damage that might have ensued.

Psalm 119 gives us a glimpse of a person who spiritually prepares for the future. To prevent the damage from sin, it depicts a person both treasuring and storing God's Word in their heart. In the original rendering of this verse, the concept of both treasuring and storing Scripture is from a single Hebrew word, *tsaphan*. Upon studying it, I can see why it is not easily translated to one simple word.

Tsaphan on one level means to hide up, save, treasure, or store. But it doesn't stop there. It also portrays the acts of lurking, stealthily watching, and ambushing![1] When we roll it all into one, we see just what having our hearts armed with the Word of God can do to sin.

Scripture treasured and stored in our hearts can be called to memory when we need it. It aids us in defending against Satan's schemes, and it also can assist us in combating any thoughts and desires we might have that would not please God. We can stand armed and ready to pull out the weapon of the Word when we feel tempted, just as Jesus did in the wilderness (Matthew 4:1–11).

Some of the heartache in life comes from the wrong and sinful choices we make. The fallout of such choices finds us anxious and regretful. But we can purpose to prepare for the storms and temptations that lie ahead. We can not only read and study our Bibles, but we can also commit important verses to memory.

Let's prepare for the times of testing that will inevitably come. Let's treasure God's Word enough to store it up in our minds and hearts, being ready to rely on its power in times of turmoil or temptation.

POINTS TO PONDER

Identify a time when you recalled Scripture in facing a temptation.

_____

_____

_____

_____

What are some goals you have when it comes to memorizing God's Word?

_____

_____

_____

_____

_____

PAUSING TO PRAY

Heavenly Father, *I want to be prepared to combat the temptation to sin. One verse I would like to memorize is* _____

_____

_____

_____

35 | Be Careful

Ruth

Scripture to Study

Be very careful, then, how you live—not as unwise but as wise.

Ephesians 5:15

I am struck with how often I can remember as a child my parents or grandparents instructing me to "be careful." Sometimes it was because the stove was hot. Or I was riding my bike. As I grew older, it was the wisdom offered before returning to my college campus. And then the first steps *I* was taking as a mom.

In all of these situations, and in countless others, it was always for my good. It was for my protection and my flourishing.

"Be careful."

It's not surprising, then, as we turn to God's Word, how often we are lovingly warned to do the same. The heart of God is revealed in the Fatherhood of God. He has saved us and called us into relationship with himself. He is a Father who loves his kids. And to follow in the footsteps of his Son is the path forward to the good life, the abundant life. But in order to increasingly experience this flourishing life in Christ, we have to learn to pay attention and keep our eyes open. We have to be alert. We have to "be careful," as Ephesians 5:15 warns, with how we live.

In its context, the apostle Paul has just reminded the followers of Jesus in Ephesus that they have been saved out of an old life. They were once "darkness" (Ephesians 5:8), but now they are "light in the Lord" (v. 9). They have a new orientation—a new Center. Jesus is Savior and Lord. Rescuer and Ruler.

This new reality of having been set apart by Christ to live a new life for Christ is what motivates Paul to write and warn them, "Be very careful, then, how you live—not as unwise but as wise" (Ephesians 5:15).

Be skillful in your actions. Guarded with your decisions. Make sure you are paying attention, day in and day out, one step after another, with doing God's will. Keep your eyes on Jesus with your time. Keep in step with God's Spirit, allowing him to crucify and control your desires. Give yourself, your marriage, and your family fully to God.

"Be careful."

God does not ask us to walk through life fearful, but he does ask us to walk through life wisely. And it is always for our good and for his glory.

POINTS TO PONDER

Where do you sense God asking you to be more careful and spiritually awake?

_____

It is easy to become relaxed or to fall asleep spiritually. This is why we are routinely instructed to persevere and to pay attention. In what ways will being more careful and attentive impact the decisions you will make today?

_____

_____

_____

PAUSING TO PRAY

Father, *today I will be careful with* _____

_____

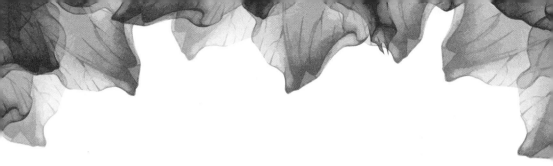

36 | Filling Up with Praise

Karen

Scripture to Study

My mouth is full of praise and honor to you all day long.

Psalm 71:8 CSB

Recently I received as a gift a newfangled teakettle, and I use it almost every day. Rather than being made of metal and whistling to me when ready from on top of the stove, this one is a glass vessel that has an electric base and plugs into the outlet in my kitchen. The best-loved feature about my new appliance is that it automatically shuts off when the water has boiled. No more boiling the teakettle dry! (Not that that's ever happened to anyone I know—wink, wink!)

But this whistling glass contraption isn't completely foolproof. The manufacturer makes it clear in the accompanying owner's manual that the most important aspect of operating the kettle is to never let the water go below the minimum fill line, which is clearly marked on the side. If it does, you will burn out the heating element of the pot, ruining it for good. So before selecting my favorite bag of fruity herbal tea and firing up the kettle, I make sure the water level is way above that lowest fill line.

At times in our walk with the Lord, we feel rather low on faith and trust. Our souls become depleted and our countenance falls. We need to be filled back up. At such times, there is one practice that seems to raise my spiritual level more quickly than anything else. It is the practice of praise.

Psalm 71 is one that describes God's help—even to those who are in their older years. Verse 8 (CSB) depicts the actions of such a person who needs assistance:

My mouth is full of praise and honor to you all day long.

I find it hard to pout when my heart is filled with praise. And when we, like the writer of this portion of Scripture, intentionally fill our mouths with praise and honor throughout the day, we can more effectively focus on the goodness of God. Recalling God's goodness—thanking and praising him for it—soon refills our souls, ushering in hope and imparting peace.

We can praise God inwardly:

> Praise the LORD, my soul;
> all my inmost being, praise his holy name.
> Psalm 103:1

We can praise him before the multitudes:

> Give praise to the LORD, proclaim his name;
> make known among the nations what he has done.
> Psalm 105:1

We can praise the Lord when we are sad or distraught:

> Why, my soul, are you downcast?
> Why so disturbed within me?
> Put your hope in God,
> for I will yet praise him,
> my Savior and my God
> Psalm 42:11

Our praise to God can go on without end:

> I will exalt you, my God the King;
> I will praise your name for ever and ever.
> Psalm 145:1

Don't let your soul run low on praise. Fill it back up by remembering in your heart—and telling with your mouth—all the wonderful attributes of God.

> Let everything that has breath praise the LORD.
> Praise the LORD.
>
> Psalm 150:6

POINTS TO PONDER

Take a few moments right now to ponder the goodness of God. Write out a few sentences of praise to him. Don't focus on your circumstances. Center your soul on all the wonderful attributes of God.

_____

_____

_____

_____

_____

PAUSING TO PRAY

Gracious Father, *I thank you for never leaving my side. Today I specifically praise you for* _____

_____

_____

_____

37 | Beyond Remorse

Ruth

> ## Scripture to Study
>
> When Judas, who had betrayed him, saw that Jesus was condemned, he was seized with remorse and returned the thirty pieces of silver to the chief priests and the elders. "I have sinned," he said, "for I have betrayed innocent blood."
>
> Matthew 27:3–4

What would you do over again if you could?

We probably all have a long list of things we feel remorse over. A word spoken with the barbwire of our anger. A decision we can't get back but we keep rewinding again and again. We look in the rearview mirror of previous relationships and see the carnage of friends and family we've wounded with our pride and self-righteousness. Who hasn't done or said something they wish they could do over?

If only I could . . .

I wish I would have . . .

I know I shouldn't have . . .

Why did I say . . .

Perhaps one of the best biblical examples of remorse is Judas. He's often referred to in the Bible as the "betrayer." He is, after all, deserving of the title. The Gospels tell us he turned against Jesus, forsaking him, betraying him for thirty pieces of silver.

He's not the only one to do so. Peter did the same. But while their betrayal may have been similar, their response was entirely different. In Matthew 27, we get a glimpse into Judas's deep sorrow over his sin.

Clearly Judas felt remorse. And deep sorrow. But the difference is that remorse can fall short. Remorse can often focus on us—on how *we* have sinned instead of on *whom* we have sinned against. Remorse can be me-centered; repentance is God-centered. Remorse or regret fails to take the failure to God.

Peter moved beyond remorse to repentance. And when he did, he was met with God's unconditional love and forgiveness. So here is the good news, friends: When you fail, you have a Father who has forgiven you in Christ. His kindness leads us to repentance, not just remorse. He wants us to come to him, the real object of our offense, but also the real source of our healing and hope.

POINTS TO PONDER

Why is it sometimes so difficult to move from remorse to repentance?

_____

_____

Remorse can often focus on ways we have fallen short. Repentance is focused on how we have sinned against the One who loves us the most. In what area(s) of your life do you need to move from remorse to repentance?

_____

_____

_____

PAUSING TO PRAY

Father, you have called me into freedom and intimacy. I not only regret my sin, but I repent of _____

_____

38 | When You Need to Cast Your Cares

Karen

When our children were all small, my husband and I took them to an aquatic theme park for the day. There were waterslides and wading pools and roller coasters that slowly climbed up a steep incline only to plunge forcefully down into the water, soaking everyone in sight. The kids quickly darted from ride to ride, enjoying both the warm sunshine and the cool sprays of water.

I was looking forward to this trip because our children were getting older, which meant no one needed to be carted about in a stroller anymore. The thought of walking without pushing that contraption made me smile. That is, until my children decided that all the sundries they were accumulating were too much for them to carry. Since my husband is the fun dad who never misses accompanying them on any ride, I became the carryall, loaded down with their sunglasses, juice boxes, and souvenirs from the gift shop.

The kids handed their items to me almost instinctively. The minute we approached the next ride, they turned to me, quickly unloaded their items, and then ran off happily to play, trusting me with their things.

Throughout life, we encounter various twists and turns. The uncertainty of what lies ahead often finds us burdened with cares. However, just as 1 Peter 5:7 states, we can cast our cares upon the Lord, knowing he cares for us deeply. We can hand him our troubles and launch back into life secure in the knowledge that he has our best interests at heart. It should be second nature, trusting God in all the things. But oh, is this easier said than done!

The Amplified version of this verse gives us greater insight into both how and why we cast our cares upon Christ. We don't just pick and choose which ones we will bring to him, not wanting to bother him with those that are too small or others that are too great. No. Read the bracketed deeper meaning again:

Casting all your cares [all your anxieties, all your worries, and all your concerns, once and for all].

How glorious! *All* means . . . *all!* And we do it once and for all, not checking back in every minute to see how he is handling them.

The remainder of the verse gives us our why—the reason we can confidently hand our cares off to Jesus. Because "He cares about you [with deepest affection, and watches over you very carefully]." The Greek words translated as "cares about you" indicate having deep concern about someone, taking an interest in or paying careful attention to a person's welfare. The Lord is ever mindful of our burdens and wants to relieve us from shouldering the weight of them alone. He is waiting for us to trust and release and then forge ahead carefree.

Is it time you turned to your Father and handed him that which you have been carrying for too long? He is ready to take it from you, granting your mind assurance and your heart true peace.

POINTS TO PONDER

What is a current burden you are carrying that you need to hand off to the Lord?

_____

_____

How might knowing the deeper meaning of 1 Peter 5:7 help you to do this?

_____

_____

_____

_____

_____

─── **PAUSING TO PRAY** ───

Dear Father, *I'm tired of trying to carry the weight of my burdens alone. Today, I commit to* _____

_____

_____

_____

39 | The Secret Life

Ruth

Scripture to Study

No one who wants to become a public figure acts in secret. Since you are doing these things, show yourself to the world.

John 7:4

It seems like everywhere we look, everybody is trying to be somebody. We especially see it on social media, where fans are made and followers are enlisted for just about anything under the sun!

- Fashion
- Dancing
- Fitness
- Food
- Travel
- Music
- And more

Of course, all social media is not bad. But what it can reveal is our human need to be seen. We all desire others to know us, see us, and love us. This is why we have to be so careful and wise when it comes to what we do and why we do it.

It seems that even Jesus' brothers fell into this trap. As Jesus' popularity was growing, they wanted others to see him. The hidden life was not enough. John tells us that as the Feast of Tabernacles was approaching, they encouraged Jesus to come out of hiding!

Jesus' brothers said to him, "Leave Galilee and go to Judea, so that your disciples there may see the works you do. No one who wants to become a public figure acts in secret. Since you are doing these things, show yourself to the world." For even his own brothers did not believe in him.

John 7:3–5

Jesus would indeed become a public figure. But not in the way they thought. And not in their timing. He had come to do one thing—obey his Father's will. This eventually would lead to his being publicly lifted up as Savior and King of the World. A crucified Messiah. A Suffering Servant.

"No one who wants to become a public figure acts in secret," we read. But how much do we desire to be a "private figure"? Do we seek first the kingdom of God, whether people see it or not? How much do we hunger and thirst to do the small things, the things no one sees, when no one is looking?

No matter who sees or notices you, remember you have a Father "who sees what is done in secret," and the promise Jesus gives is that he will "reward you" (Matthew 6:4).

POINTS TO PONDER

In what area(s) of your life do you struggle most with being seen by others?

_____

We can often be motivated by what others think of us. And yet Jesus taught that the motivation of our heart should be to honor God, whether others see it or not. He is our great Reward and his approval matters most. Do you believe that? Is the truth that God sees you enough?

PAUSING TO PRAY

Father, I will honor you in secret by _____

40 | Drop the Security Blanket

Karen

Scripture to Study

And the angel said unto them, Fear not: for, behold, I bring you good tidings of great joy, which shall be to all people. For unto you is born this day in the city of David a Saviour, which is Christ the Lord.

Luke 2:10–11 KJV

In 1965, the holiday classic *A Charlie Brown Christmas* TV special was released. There is a memorable scene in which the character Linus, holding that signature security blanket of his, delivers a speech telling of the true meaning of Christmas. Linus, who was never once drawn by artist Charles Schulz without his security blanket, begins delivering that speech with the blanket in hand, sometimes holding it to look like a shepherd's crook. The passage, Luke 2:8–14, includes this announcement:

> Fear not: for, behold, I bring you good tidings of great joy, which shall be to all people. For unto you is born this day in the city of David a Saviour, which is Christ the Lord.
>
> (vv. 10–11)

There is a crucial detail that makes the clip extremely relevant, and which many people claim was subtly, but purposefully, put in by Mr. Schulz. Linus releases his beloved security blanket during his speech. The audience is shocked. This kid never let go of his blanket! Ever. But he did now. And just when did he drop it? Precisely at the time he utters the phrase "Fear not"!

In real life, true security is found only when we drop what we have been holding on to tightly and falsely relying on, and instead trust our God who tells us to "fear not."

In Luke 2:9, we read that when the angel came upon the shepherds, "they were sore afraid." The phrase "sore afraid" is translated from the Greek word *phobeó*, which comes from the root word *phobos*. Does it make you think of another English word? Yes, the word *phobia*.

The English definition of *phobia* is a strong fear, or dislike of someone or something. It is an uncontrollable dread that may be abnormal or even irrational. *Phobeó* paints an even more vivid picture. It means "to be struck with fear, to be seized with alarm,"[1] to dread or fear harm or injury, "to put to flight by terrifying (to scare away)."[2]

When the shepherds were "sore afraid," the angel told them to "fear not." They could rest in security, knowing Christ was now with them.

We today have Christ with us. He has granted us access to God. This is what will bring us security—security that no person, possession, or position can ever provide. We find refuge in spending time in God's Word, tethering our hearts to it as we dive in deep, not just reading it—as important as that is—but studying it, committing it to memory, and then living by its principles, precepts, and commands.

Let's find our security in Jesus alone.

POINTS TO PONDER

What person, possessions, or positions in your life have you been holding on to for security, rather than clinging to God?

_____

_____

_____

_____

_____

How does knowing that God alone provides the ultimate security help you not to fear?

_____

_____

_____

_____

_____

PAUSING TO PRAY

Father, I want to let go of my greatest fears and find my security with you. Help me get rid of the false security of _____

_____

_____

_____

41 | The Downward Life

Ruth

Scripture to Study

In your relationships with one another, have the same mindset as Christ Jesus: Who, being in very nature God, did not consider equality with God something to be used to his own advantage; rather, he made himself nothing by taking the very nature of a servant, being made in human likeness.

Philippians 2:5–7

Have you ever noticed how Jesus moved downward in his life? Jesus, the eternal Son of God, took on flesh, in what is known as the incarnation (John 1:1–4). The humility of God is expressed in the taking on of humanity by God.

Jesus, the God-man, moved downward in his earthly ministry.

- The Son becomes a son.
- The eternal One wraps himself in flesh.
- The One who demands obedience becomes obedient, even to death on a cross.
- Highly exalted, he is humiliated.
- Worthy of worship, Jesus is abandoned, misunderstood, mocked, and crucified.

Why? For you. For me. For us. The downward, self-giving, and sacrificial life of Jesus flows from the heart of Jesus. He descends so that we might encounter the love of God. And that love might change us and pour out through us.

The apostle Paul, when he was writing to a group of Jesus-followers, encouraged them to do the same with one another—to give of themselves.

He commands them to honor one another in humility, in the same way Jesus loved us by lowering himself. He says we are to have the "same mindset as Christ Jesus," who "made himself nothing by taking the very nature of a servant" (Philippians 2:5–7).

This is so counter to how we live, isn't it? It confronts what we value, what we want, what we think is the good life. Our motivation is often the opposite. We want to ascend. We crave attention. Approval. Recognition.

And yet the work of God in us is so that we might increasingly turn outward. The Spirit of God is working to pry us away from our own egos. God is leading us away from ourselves and to a greater love for him and for one another. What it looks like is a downward life.

Today, as you consider all that you have to do or all that you want, will you choose to ascend or descend? What would the downward life look like for you?

POINTS TO PONDER

Where do you see the temptation in your own life to ascend?

_____

We serve a crucified Savior who models for us what the good life really looks like. While our culture might value ascending, God values descending. It is where we meet the love of God, and it is where others encounter it as well. In what ways will this perspective impact your everyday life?

_____

_____

_____

PAUSING TO PRAY

Father, give me the grace to descend by _____

42 | And All That Jazz

Karen

Scripture to Study

Your word is a lamp for my feet and a light on my path.

Psalm 119:105 CSB

My favorite social media app is Instagram. Not only do I love having it so I can see what is happening in the lives of faraway family and friends, I also love the fact that it's rather drama-free when compared with other platforms such as Twitter or Facebook. I can tap, swipe, and scroll, usually without being tempted to become entangled in a social media spat.

A few days ago, however, my happy scrolling was interrupted when I saw an ad appear on my screen. It was promoting a sale on some Bible study accessories such as colorful highlighters, trendy bookmarks, and a set of whimsical tabs for all sixty-six books of the Bible. These products looked whimsical and even helpful. But what stood out to me most was the tease at the top of the post. It told readers that it was about time they jazzed up their Bibles.

Now, of course the entrepreneur of these items was talking about adding functionality and even a little color to your physical Bible. Instead, I thought of this saying in a spiritual sense, how so often in our culture we try to jazz up God's Word. We display Scripture on a lovely social media graphic or on a rustically stenciled sign for our home. While there is nothing wrong with using Scripture in our decorating—whether in home or online—let's remember what the purpose of Scripture is in the first place.

The writer of Psalm 119 declared that God's Word is a lamp for our feet and a light on our path. A lamp in ancient Bible times was used to help you find your way in the dark. You held it over your feet as you walked along a pathway. This illumination helped keep you from stumbling and falling.

The original Hebrew meaning of the items depicted in this verse—a lamp, feet, and a light—are straightforward. Their English meanings match. However, the phrase *Your word* has a multifaceted meaning that we would do well to pay attention to.

The Hebrew connotation for *word* can be all of the following: a message, commands, edicts, advice, thoughts, verdicts, conversation, counsel, and promises. Isn't this myriad of meanings remarkable?!

Do you need advice? *Go to God's Word.*

Would you like to know God's thoughts? *His Word lights the way.*

Could you use a good conversation with Jesus today? *You will find it on the pages of Scripture.* Want to be sure you are following the Lord's commands? *Crack open your Bible.*

And if you'd like to explore the promises of God, *you will find them lovingly penned on its pages.*

Our Bibles don't need to be jazzed up at all. They need to be diligently read, carefully studied, and their commands prayerfully applied. Let God's holy Word light your path and show you the way forward. May it illuminate your mind, causing you to eliminate ungodly behavior.

Make an appointment to encounter Jesus through God's Word very soon. (Cute Instagram picture of said meeting is optional.)

POINT TO PONDER

Which of the various meanings for *word* in the Hebrew language most speaks to you today and why?

_____

_____

PAUSING TO PRAY

Almighty God, I want your Word to be what guides my life. When it comes to studying my Bible, a goal that I have is _____

_____

43 | Loving Others in Your Pain

Ruth

Scripture to Study

When Jesus saw his mother there, and the disciple whom he loved standing nearby, he said to her, "Woman, here is your son," and to the disciple; "Here is your mother." From that time on, this disciple took her into his home.

John 19:26–27

I sat alone, as I often did, in the waiting room. It was a follow-up from my last miscarriage. While the wait time seemed like an eternity, the weight I was carrying felt enormous. Everyone around me looked so happy. Their news was so very different from mine. Not only did I sit alone, but I felt very alone.

I could feel my pain pulling me inward. My mind couldn't help but think about some of the calls I wish I had received from friends over the past few weeks. Or visits. I had plenty of people to love and support me, but I was battling that sneaky temptation to turn *inward* in my pain.

Do you know what I mean? Those deceptive thoughts like, *Does anyone really care?* or, *I wish someone would . . .*

It's easy to allow our pain to consume us, isn't it? And even to cloud the way we see God and relate to others. We all need appropriate boundaries at times, seasons of healing, and an abundance of God's grace to put us back together. We need the Spirit of God to give us the Father's love, but we all need the Holy Spirit to help us turn toward others—even in our pain.

This is one of the beautiful, yet challenging, examples in Jesus' life. Even in his suffering, he is still sacrificing. John tells us that on the cross, Jesus is still thinking of others—entrusting his mother into the care of his disciples.

What does it look like for us to follow in our Savior's footsteps? It looks like allowing our pain to soften, not harden, our heart toward others. It looks like offering our wounds as fertile soil for God to grow compassion toward one another.

If we don't begin, with God's help, to think and act toward others in our pain, our pain will eventually define us.

Maybe turning outward means beginning to pray for someone you know is struggling.

It means sending the first text message.

Making the first phone call.

Instead of waiting, asking to get together for coffee or lunch.

My prayer for you today, friend, is that God would give you the grace to begin turning to others, even in small ways, in your pain. This is what Jesus did as he poured out love for others, even in his darkest moment. May he give you the desire to use your own pain for the good of someone else—namely to help them draw closer to God and experience his great and healing love.

POINTS TO PONDER

What are some small or simple ways you can begin turning outward instead of inward in your pain?

_____

_____

Turning outward in our pain is never something we do in our own strength. As you meditate on the love of Christ, ask him to give you his heart of compassion toward others, even in your suffering. Write down the names of a few hurting people you will reach out to this week.

_____

_____

_____

PAUSING TO PRAY

Father, *Lover of my soul, help me to love others by* _____

_____

_____

_____

_____

_____

_____

_____

44 | If This, Then That

Karen

Scripture to Study

Commit your activities to the LORD,
and your plans will be established.

Proverbs 16:3 CSB

Last week, all three of our adult children were at our home for a visit. As it often does when they are together, the conversation turned to memorable—and oftentimes funny—recollections of their childhood.

During this get-together, one of the siblings accused another one of eating the last piece of rhubarb crisp that they had already claimed for themself. And then, in a blast from the past, they called out, "Double restitution!" This phrase was taken from a handmade chart that hung on our kitchen wall that spelled out some of our family's personal policies. Dubbed the "If This . . . Then That" chart, it gave the consequences for certain behaviors.

For example, if a family member hurt someone's feelings—whether on purpose or unintentionally—then they were required to apologize. However, it could not done be with a one-word "Sorry," but only by thoroughly completing the statement, "I am sorry for_____." So if you caused wounded feelings, then you apologized completely.

The shout of "Double restitution!" was voiced between these now-grown siblings because this was a consequence for any stealing. If you snuck a dollar out of your brother's Batman wallet, you then owed him two dollars. This was the If This . . . Then That consequence for that offense.

Psalm 16:3 seems to have its own version of If This . . . Then That. However, it's not spelling out a punishment; it's giving us a promise!

> Commit your activities to the LORD,
> and your plans will be established.

Doesn't our human behavior sometimes showcase quite the opposite? We establish our plans, making them on our own. Then we decide to commit them to the Lord, enlisting his help in carrying them to completion. What instead is this verse calling us to do?

Time for a little ancient vocab lesson. The Hebrew word for *commitment* is *galal*. It means simply "to roll." Our English word for *activities* comes from the Hebrew word *maaseh*, which is translated as "work, deeds, or actions." The original term for *plans—machashabah—*has several shades of meaning including "actions, thoughts, ways, plots, or schemes." Finally, our shortest vocab word for *established* is *kun*, and is translated as "firm, certain, ordained, or rested."

And so, if our assignment in English class today was to craft a clear explanation using all these words, we might say that when we roll our actions and work to the Lord, he will help us to make our thoughts and ways firmly rooted in him, and we can rest in certainty as we carry them out.

Let's ponder the concept of rolling for a second. If you roll a ball to someone, do you keep your hands on it? No. It's impossible to grasp a ball tightly and still roll it to someone. This illustration helps me better understand my own thoughts, ways, work, and deeds. We can trustingly hand them off to God, deciding through prayer what our steps should be, and running them through the grid of God's Word, discovering if they are in keeping with what would please him.

If we commit our activities to the Lord in this manner, *then* our plans will be firmly established, according to him, and the outcome will not find us full of regret.

POINTS TO PONDER

How does Proverbs 16:3 challenge or encourage you when it comes to making your plans in life?

_____

_____

What is one action step you will take in this area to make your planning align with the instructions in this verse?

_____

_____

_____

_____

PAUSING TO PRAY

Heavenly Father, *help me to roll my plans to you today about*

_____

_____

_____

_____

_____

45 | Surrendering Expectations

Ruth

Scripture to Study

When John, who was in prison, heard about the deeds of the Messiah, he sent his disciples to ask him, "Are you the one who is to come, or should we expect someone else?"

Matthew 11:2–3

It was a good question. An honest one. Especially since everything John the Baptist thought was going to be true of the Messiah didn't seem to be matching his current reality.

The Gospel of Matthew first mentions John being put in prison in Matthew 4:12. Now in Matthew 11, as Jesus is continuing to teach his disciples, John sends his disciples to ask Jesus his question.

"Are you the one who is to come, or should we expect someone else?" (Matthew 11:3).

There's that word—*expect*. John knew the Scriptures. Most likely what John has in mind is all of the expectations of the Messiah, in particular the prophecies in the Old Testament book of Isaiah. Expectations about good news for the poor, healing for the brokenhearted, setting captives free, favor from the Lord, and comfort for those who mourn (Isaiah 61:1–2).

The problem, and the motivation behind the question, is that much of John's current reality was not matching his expectations. After all, he was in prison because of his righteousness. So John asks a question we probably all ask when we are struggling to trust God. The question we all ask when things seem out of our control. Or maybe the question we all ask when God is not behaving as we think he should or expect him to be.

Jesus' response to John is one we all need. He assures John that there is no contradiction between what God's Word says and what he is currently experiencing. Not all of John's expectations—or at least the timing of them—are correct. But God's purposes are right on track. So don't lose heart. Don't give up.

Jesus' encouraging answer to John's question was that "what you hear" is correct: The healings are happening. The good news is being preached. The true Messiah has come (Matthew 11:4–6). He can be trusted.

I so need this reminder in my own life. When my own expectations are not meeting my current reality, God's purposes have not failed. His love for me has not ceased. His goodness toward me is not stingy. It might look different. Feel different. But God has not abandoned me; he is still with me and for me.

POINTS TO PONDER

How is your current reality different from your expectations?

_____

Jesus wants to assure you today that he is still with you and for you. When our experience of God does not match our expectation of God, it is not evidence of the absence of God. Take some time to list the specific circumstances you will hand over to him today.

_____

_____

_____

PAUSING TO PRAY

Father, I will continue to trust you even though _____

_____

46 | Pursuing Diverse Relationships

Karen

Scripture to Study

Grace to you and peace from God our Father and the Lord Jesus Christ.

Philippians 1:2 csb

I stroll out to our mailbox each afternoon. Normally, it's stuffed with junk mail. However, every so often, I retrieve an envelope that puts a spring in my step. What is this joy-inducing item? A handwritten note.

Today we tend to communicate by texting or direct messages on social media, getting right to the point without a flowery introduction. But an old-fashioned letter begins with a friendly opener. (Anyone else recall writing out possible "salutations" for a letter in English class?)

The author of Philippians, the apostle Paul, used two welcoming words in his opening: *grace* and *peace*. If we do our history homework, we discover that Paul wasn't merely choosing two friendly salutations from a list he'd learned in an ancient classroom. His greeting was rather deliberate. He was seeking to be inclusive in a culture that was often segregated.

In the New Testament civilization, the term *grace* was customarily used when greeting a Gentile—anyone who was not of Jewish heritage. The Greek word translated as "grace" here is *charis*, and at its core denotes displaying joy, pleasure, beauty, and brightness.

The word *peace* was normally spoken or written when one was talking to someone who was a Jew. The original word is *eirene*. This type of peace isn't just one that means an absence of worrisome conditions; it means comprehensive well-being. The church body at Philippi was comprised of Jews and non-Jews, and right out of the chute, Paul included them both. By using both the words *grace* and *peace* in his inaugural

127

greeting, Paul is echoing what we read in Galatians 3:28: "There is nei-ther Jew nor Gentile, neither slave nor free, nor is there male and female, for you are all one in Christ Jesus."

This group of Christ-followers was diverse in other ways too. It con-tained people of different socioeconomic statuses. Additionally, Paul's acknowledgment of—and friendship with—a woman named Lydia was a bold statement of the gender inclusiveness of the gospel in a culture where women were often overlooked and marginalized. (Read more about Lydia in Acts 16.)

All this makes me wonder, are we trusting God to help us pursue diverse relationships? Would a quick scroll through the contact lists in our phones show that we are friends with only those who look and live much like we do? Or would we spy people of various colors and ethnicities, and from assorted walks of life?

Challenge yourself to choose those you might not normally befriend in real life—those who don't look or live like you do. You may just make someone's day, the way I'm sure Paul's kind opening words did for both Jew and Gentile.

May we take a cue from Philippians and reach out in love to pursue diverse relationships, trusting God to help us display the gospel as we do.

POINT TO PONDER

How, specifically, might the Lord be prompting you to become more inclusive today?

_____

_____

PAUSING TO PRAY

Father, help me discover ways to reach out to others who do not look and live like I do. I desire to _____

_____

47 | Making Room for God

Ruth

Scripture to Study

Lord, our Lord, how majestic is your name in all the earth!

Psalm 8:1

was up early. Long before any of our kids were awake. So I did what I always do—executed my typical morning routine.

- Fed the dog.
- Made coffee.
- Prayed.
- Then read my Bible.

When I was done, it was still early. And somehow, our kids were still not awake! This meant a little more time for me. So I decided to go for a walk.

The sun was just beginning to peek its nose above the clouds to the east of our neighborhood. Spring was just shrugging off the remnants of winter in Michigan. The sounds and smells felt especially fresh that early morning.

As I finished that first lap around our neighborhood, I began to think about the psalmist's words in Psalm 8:1, "Lord, our Lord, how majestic is your name in all the earth!" I kept rolling that word *majestic* around and around in my mouth—sort of like a juicy morsel you are enjoying and don't want to swallow quite yet!

How majestic are you, O Lord. *Majestic* is a word that is used in a variety of ways throughout the Bible. It can mean powerful or famous or excellent. One could say of kings or nations, "How mighty are you."

But here the psalmist is saying how "majestic" are the character and actions of our God "in all the earth."

I was struck that morning with how often I try to *move* God instead of *make room for* God. Not that these are always opposed to one another. It's just that often we can try to get our way. Force our will. Tell God what we want. We want to move God.

Are we content to make room for God? Do we just delight in him? Revel in his majesty? Adore the Lord? Worship him? To make room for God is to love him and be loved by him. It is to wait on the Lord, listening for his voice to speak so that *we* might be moved by *him*.

May we increasingly make room for our majestic God who is near us and in control. He can be trusted in all the things. He is mighty not only in our life, but in "all the earth!" It is what we know to be true of the Lord that allows us to trust our God in all the things.

POINTS TO PONDER

What is the difference between trying to "move God" and "making room for God"?

_____

It is not wrong to bring our needs to God and ask him to act on our behalf. But God also desires that we make room for him, carving out time to just be with him. What are a few simple ways you can begin to intentionally make room for him?

_____

_____

PAUSING TO PRAY

Lord, you are majestic because _____

_____

48 | Flawed and Yet Useful

Karen

Scripture to Study

So I went down to the potter's house, and there he was, working away at the wheel. But the jar that he was making from the clay became flawed in the potter's hand, so he made it into another jar, as it seemed right for him to do.

Jeremiah 18:3–4 CSB

Living in our current digital age has made so many processes easier. For example, we can order groceries to be left at our front door or get dinner for the family by simply typing into an app that will trigger a delivery person to bring it to us still piping hot. But perhaps the app for securing items I most use is Facebook Marketplace. It's like a perpetual worldwide garage sale at the tip of my fingers!

I often tease that our home is decorated in mid-century Facebook Marketplace. I secured a retro plant stand for our living room, a vintage china hutch for the dining area, and the large pine executive desk where I now sit writing these words. The great prices and ease of shopping are so much better than hauling myself around to garage sales and antique auctions like I used to back in the day.

Recently, I was on the hunt for a new canning kettle to use for preserving homemade salsa or putting up raspberry jam to give as Christmas gifts to friends and neighbors. I hopped on the site and typed the words *canning kettle* in the search bar. Up popped several options from which I could choose. The one that most caught my eye had a super low price, looked to be in great shape, and came with a rack to hold the Mason jars. In the description I read, "Nearly new, but with a slight blemish on the lid. Blemish does not affect the usefulness of the pot."

I snatched it up, and my newly acquired canning kettle turns out the most delicious jams, jellies, and other preserved fruits and veggies. And the seller was right. The imperfection does not at all affect the effectiveness of the pot.

The prophet Jeremiah observed a potter at work at the wheel and announced the "the jar that he was making from the clay became flawed in the potter's hand, so he made it into another jar, as it seemed right for him to do."

Spiritually speaking, God is the Potter, and we are the clay. Isaiah 64:8 affirms this: "Yet LORD, you are our Father; we are the clay, and you are our potter; we all are the work of your hands."

Our God, the Creator of all things, knows us utterly and completely. While we may look at a blemish we possess in our personality and fear it may disqualify us from being effective, God can take that same flaw and transform it, allowing us to become a vessel that is useful for the kingdom.

May we humbly offer our flaws up to the Lord. What we see as a blemish can be beautiful in his sight if we are willing to allow him to tenderly rework us from the inside out.

POINTS TO PONDER

Do you have a perceived blemish in your personality makeup that often frustrates you?

How might the image of the potter in today's devotion help you to see this differently?

_____

_____

PAUSING TO PRAY

Creative and loving Father of all, please take what I view as a blemish and _____

49 | The Apple of God's Eye

Ruth

> ### Scripture to Study
>
> In a desert land he found him,
>   in a barren and howling waste.
> He shielded him and cared for him;
>   he guarded him as the apple of his eye.
>
> Deuteronomy 32:10

When we think of Moses, we typically think of him as the great lawgiver of Israel. The one who on numerous occasions climbed the mountain to meet with God. Up Moses would go, only to come down again. And for what purpose? So that God's people might be shaped and molded by the words of God and then sent out to be a different kind of people for God—a light to the nations.

But as it turns out, Moses was also a singer. Or at least we have a song recorded by him in Deuteronomy 32. Toward the end of Moses' life, we read, the Lord had instructed Moses to write down not laws this time but a song. And oddly enough, this would be a song that was meant to remind the Israelites of who they were and whose they were—though they were prone to forget and prone to wander (Deuteronomy 31:19–22).

One of the lines I love most from this song is God's reminder that we are loved by him. Or as Deuteronomy 32:10 says, we are the "apple of his eye."

It's so tempting, isn't it, to look for the approval of others? To see our worth or value in what we do or what we have. We all face the struggle to live for the gaze of someone else's eyes instead of God's.

We know God loves us, but our struggle is whether or not God's love for us is enough. In the New Testament, we see the greatest expression of God's love for us in the life, death, and resurrection of Jesus (Romans 5:8).

God's love is not something we earn; it is something we freely receive, by faith. Are you convinced of God's love for you? If not, ask him for the grace to not only believe his love, but to experience it today. You are loved by God. You really are the apple of his eye. May you not forget who you are or whose you are!

How do you most often look to someone else's eyes for worth?

_____

_____

_____

Our worth comes not from what we do but from what has been done for us in Christ. We are loved by God, and the cross is the greatest evidence that we really are the apple of God's eye. In what area(s) of your life might you be trying to earn God's love? Hand that over to him today.

_____

_____

_____

_____

---- PAUSING TO PRAY ----

Jesus, I will remember I am loved because _____

_____

_____

50 | Calm Down and Be Quiet

Karen

Scripture to Study

Say to him: Calm down and be quiet. Don't be afraid or cowardly because of these two smoldering sticks, the fierce anger of Rezin and Aram, and the son of Remaliah.

Isaiah 7:4 CSB

On those days when my heart starts to fret, I'd like to say that I quickly "put my Jesus on," taking my worries to the Lord in prayer. But if I am being honest, the first thing I typically think about is calling a friend. A few of my friends have careers in the field of counseling, and I'm always certain they will give me some great advice that will help to calm my fears.

But the words of counsel from those at the top of my contacts list aren't the only reason I want to pick up the phone to call them. It also has to do with my own words. You see, when I start to feel anxiety welling up in my heart, my lips want a piece of the action. I just can't seem to stop talking about my troubles at hand! And my poor husband. If I am not successful in reaching a friend, he must sit patiently listening as my words fly out a mile a minute, recounting to him all my woes and dire predictions about the situation that's causing me angst.

In the seventh chapter of Isaiah, we happen upon a scene where the Old Testament prophet Isaiah is giving counsel to King Ahaz. His message is one of reassurance. Even though two invading kings—Rezin and Aram, whom he refers to as smoldering sticks—are threatening, ultimately, they will not prevail.

Isaiah's script for the little pep talk begins with this five-word directive: "Calm down and be quiet" (Isaiah 7:4 CSB). The original Hebrew word *shamar* used in this verse for our English phrase *calm down* means to be careful, to watch, to take note, and to wait. And the meaning of the Hebrew *shaqat*, translated as "be quiet," is to refrain from making noise, to be peaceful, pacified, to be at rest, or to be undisturbed.

When facing trying times, our hearts and minds don't naturally go to a place of peaceful rest. We aren't elated over the watching and waiting. And our souls are far from undisturbed. But this passage isn't saying these feelings and actions are our initial and innate response. Far from it. They are thoughts and actions we must purposefully pursue.

Isaiah next delivers a second five-word TED talk: "Don't be afraid or cowardly." The English equivalent of *afraid* in Hebrew is *yare'* and the meanings in both languages line up precisely. However, the original word for *cowardly* is more nuanced. This verb—*rakak*—refers to growing soft, weak, or fainthearted.

When the anxieties and cares of life begin to make us fear—weakening our resolve and causing us to be faint of heart—may we remember the prophet's ancient advice to the king to calm down and be quiet. It worked for him, and it can benefit us today. Instead of making noise with our mouths by talking up a storm with a friend, let's decide we will wait. And watch. We will look to the Lord to find rest and discover his peace. Only when we do that will we finally find our hearts undisturbed.

Let's hit our knees before we hit the phone, taking our cares to King Jesus.

POINTS TO PONDER

When worry or anxiety begins to take up residence in your mind, what is the first thing you usually do?

_____

_____

_____

How can the words of Isaiah 7:4 help you to handle troubling times differently from now on?

_____

_____

_____

_____

_____

PAUSING TO PRAY

Dear Jesus, *the next time I am troubled by anxious thoughts, I will calm down and be quiet, remembering that you* _____

_____

_____

_____

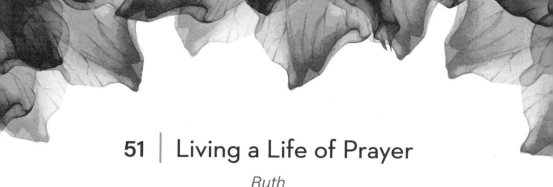

51 | Living a Life of Prayer

Ruth

Scripture to Study

Pray continually.
1 Thessalonians 5:17

There is a big difference between *living a life of prayer* and *saying prayers.*

For most of us, especially early on in our walk with Jesus, saying prayers comes first. We say a prayer in the morning. We say prayers before a meal. If we are a parent, we say prayers with our kids and for our kids. And then we say prayers before we go to bed.

As good and necessary as saying prayers can be, we soon discover that what our Father wants from us, and what he is moving us toward, is living a life of prayer. To use the apostle Paul's words in 1 Thessalonians 5:17, we are invited to "pray continually."

If you are like me, that sounds a little overwhelming! How do we pray all the time? Is God really asking us to walk around saying prayers all day, every day? Yes and no!

When we look at the life of Jesus, we get a better picture of what living a life of prayer really means. What we see in the life of Jesus is how Jesus was always in communion with the Father. Or we might say, he was always listening and obeying. He was connected to the real Source of all that is good and true and beautiful. Maybe to say it even more simply, he was in constant relationship with his Father.

Jesus wasn't focused on prayer just as an activity or something to do; he was living prayer in constant relationship with his Father. The manner, or characteristic, of Jesus' living was in prayer.

The goal for us isn't so much about trying to pray or saying prayers; the goal for us is communion or friendship with God. It's what we were created for. Prayer is the means, not the end, of communion with God. It's like an ongoing conversation that keeps us connected to the God who loves us, is with us, and is always pursuing us.

So today, don't just focus on saying prayers—live a life of prayer! Talk to God. Listen to him. Stay close to him. All day. Every day. Remember that the goal is not prayer in and of itself; the goal is friendship with God. It is satisfying and sustaining intimacy with the God who made you, loves you, and is with you!

POINTS TO PONDER

What does your prayer life look like right now?

_____

_____

Saying prayers can often be motivated by duty or obligation. Living a life of prayer is motivated by love. How can you move from saying prayers to living a life of prayer?

_____

_____

_____

PAUSING TO PRAY

Father, I want to move beyond just saying prayers. I want to live a life of prayer by _____

_____

52 | How to Want What You Have

Karen

Scripture to Study

Keep your life free from the love of money. Be satisfied with what you have, for he himself has said, I will never leave you or abandon you.

Hebrews 13:5 CSB

For most of the first two decades my husband and I were married, we struggled somewhat financially. We started out living on the combined income of his salary as a youth pastor and the wages I brought in from being a substitute teacher. But when our first child came along early in our marriage, I decided to stop working outside the home to be a full-time mom. We knew it wouldn't be easy.

Thankfully, with some ingenuity and a constant quest to penny-pinch, we made do. We used cloth diapers and I made homemade baby food—and even my own baby wipes—long before it was fashionable and plastered all over the DIY mommy Pinterest boards. It wasn't at all glamorous. Still, I wouldn't trade our family's personal decision for anything.

I'm not going to paint this frugal time in our lives in an untrue light. It was difficult. I grew envious of those who could buy new outfits or go out for a fancy dinner without even thinking about it.

Looking back on those days, I see that having to be thrifty helped us to gain an important perspective in life. We learned that true contentment isn't getting what you want; it's wanting nothing more than what you've already been given.

Hebrews 13:5 highlights this perspective. It urges, "Be satisfied with what you have, for he himself has said, I will never leave you or abandon you." Having lived through decades of having less, followed by some years of having plenty, I know from experience it's easier to keep from the love of money when you don't have a lot of money at your disposal. As Grandma used to say, you learn to use it up, wear it out, make it do, or just do without. Frugal living teaches resourcefulness, and it also can train us in contentment.

But perhaps the greatest lesson in contentment comes from the promise tethered to the tail end of that verse, the words from the Lord himself who said that he will never leave or abandon us. The Greek word translated as "leave" is *aniémi*, and its definition is to loosen, relax, let go of, or desert. Our English word *abandon* is translated from the original word *egkataleipó*, and conveys the concept of leaving behind or leaving in the lurch.

God has given us no guarantees that we will always dwell in times of financial abundance. But he has promised his abiding presence, which is the only guarantee we need in this life. Whether we are living in plenty or in want, he will never loosen his grip on us, deserting us in our lifetime on earth.

May we find our true contentment in the abundance of his presence and learn to be content with what we have.

POINTS TO PONDER

What grade would you give yourself on being free from the love of money?

What might you need to change in your perspective or your actions to be more content with what you already have?

_____

_____

PAUSING TO PRAY

Dear Jesus, I know that true contentment is found only in you. From now on, may I _____

53 | Making Time for What Matters Most

Ruth

Scripture to Study

Teach us to number our days, that we may gain a heart of wisdom.

Psalm 90:12

When my husband was recovering from his second stem cell transplant to treat his blood cancer, we dove into the world of travel. Not "real" travel, but traveling via YouTube! We would often joke, "Where do you want to go tonight? Spain? Italy? London?" This was a lot cheaper than a plane ticket and hotels!

Our entertainment, though, soon turned into dreams. Not just watching others travel but dreaming about and even making plans to travel. At least, someday. *Someday* is the key word. We don't have to be battling an illness to know that time has edges. Our someday may or may not come. This isn't meant to be depressing but to remind us to live with wisdom with the time we do have!

Just recently, my husband and I were talking about this very theme again. No matter how long we live, there will always be dreams left unfulfilled. There will always be projects not completed. There will always be places never visited. Or as I've heard it said, we will all end as "unfinished symphonies."

This is what the psalmist is reminding us of in Psalm 90. A psalm that starts out by stating God has no edges. He is not bound by time as we are. He is eternal—he always has been and always will be. What a comfort to know that he is the Unchanging One who will always be!

We, on the other hand? We are finite or limited. "Teach us to number our days," the psalmist writes in Psalm 90:12, "that we may gain a heart of wisdom." One of the things my husband said to me recently was that while none of us has time to do everything we want to do, we want to use the time we do have to invest in what matters most.

We may not travel to every continent, but are we growing in godliness?

Are we a faithful wife?

A godly mother?

A good neighbor?

Are we offering our life and our gifts in faithful service to our local church?

We are to "number our days" in order to make our days count! This is, in part, one of the secrets to not living with regret. We all have limited time, and we should take time to give ourselves to what matters most!

POINTS TO PONDER

How does counting our days lead to a heart of wisdom?

_____

_____

We number or count our days so that we make our days count. The psalmist is reminding us to live backward by thinking about the end of our lives. This helps us to live forward in the time God has graciously given us, with wisdom. How will you live differently with this in mind?

_____

_____

_____

PAUSING TO PRAY

Father, *give me a heart that wants what you want. I want to use my time to invest in* _____

_____

54 | Never Out of Sight

Karen

Scripture to Study

In peace I will lie down and sleep,
    for you alone, O Lord, will keep me safe.

Psalm 4:8 NLT

In my work-from-home routine, you can typically find me within our four walls, unless I am traveling for a speaking engagement. My husband builds cars at a local factory and, although he is on what is referred to as the day shift, he gets up at dark o'clock each morning to leave for work, sometimes before the clock strikes 4 a.m.

Lately there have been some early morning break-ins around our tiny little town, usually occurring between two and five. We felt it would be wise to have a security system in place for that stretch of time when my husband had already left for the day but I was still asleep. So after reading up on reviews and watching for a rock-bottom sale, we purchased a system and installed it.

At first, I found it a little annoying, honestly. Each time I went in or out one of our main doors, it would trigger a musical sound. When I opened a window, a different sound would chime. There is a camera and a speaker in our living room so both my husband and I can view in real time what is happening there. Sometimes, when I am at home and my husband is on break at work, he just starts talking to me through that speaker when I'm typing away on my laptop. The first time he did, it startled me. I asked him, "Hey, just how long have you been spying on me?"

Even though it now seems like I am being watched and my every move monitored by the system, I do rest more assured knowing that if someone were to try to get in while I was asleep, not only would I be alerted, but their image would be captured on camera so we would know just who they were.

Even better than the most highly rated security system, the Lord himself provides us with security, allowing us to slumber in peace. Psalm 4:8 declares, "In peace I will lie down and sleep, for you alone, O Lord, will keep me safe" (NLT). The meaning of peace in the ancient Hebrew language is completeness, soundness, safety, or well-being. And notice it isn't found in some slick security system, or even through another human. It is found in God alone.

Do you ever have trouble sleeping because of worry or anxious thoughts? Does your mind concoct all sorts of scenarios of what might go wrong in the life of a friend or loved one? Does peace seem to elude you because you fear something awful is lurking on the horizon?

Turn the words of Psalm 4:8 into a heartfelt and sincere prayer, asking the Lord to assure you of his desire to keep you safe and his willingness to be the only One who can grant you peace, allowing you to experience deep sleep.

You can't make a move without his knowing. He is ever watchful over you with his protective and loving eyes. Rest in peacefulness, dear one. The Lord won't ever let you out of his sight.

POINTS TO PONDER

Is there something keeping you awake at night? Don't ignore it; name it and then make it a matter of prayer to God.

_____

What specifically might you ask of God when it comes to this worry?

_____

_____

_____

PAUSING TO PRAY

Creator of life, tonight when my head hits the pillow and I try to drift off to sleep, help me to remember _____

_____

_____

_____

_____

_____

55 | Big Small Things

Ruth

Scripture to Study

Though it is the smallest of all seeds, yet when it grows, it is the largest of garden plants and becomes a tree, so that the birds come and perch in its branches.

Matthew 13:32

The way of Jesus seems so backward. We're into being seen; he applauds the unseen. We aspire to greatness; he calls us to be a servant. We like big things; he tells us to do small things.

In the middle of Matthew's gospel, in chapter 13, we see a transition. Leading up to chapter 13, there is a growing division between those who receive Jesus' teachings and those who don't (11:20–24). We see the religious leaders begin to conspire against him, plotting his death (12:14). And so, it is against this bubbling drama and division that Jesus begins to speak in parables.

A parable is simply a story that is meant to help a listener not only understand a point but make a decision about God and his kingdom. In Matthew 13, Jesus tells a series of short parables about God's work in the world.

He says in Matthew 13:31–32, "The kingdom of heaven is like a mustard seed, which a man took and planted in his field. Though it is the smallest of all seeds, yet when it grows, it is the largest of garden plants and becomes a tree, so that the birds come and perch in its branches." He then goes on to tell another very similar parable. This time about a woman who takes a teeny tiny amount of yeast and mixes it into a massive amount of dough! (See Matthew 13:33.)

What's the point with this parable? We tend to despise small things; Jesus delights in them. God's work in the world, Jesus is reminding us, often starts out small. It is many times unseen. Not perceptible, let alone celebrated all the time. Yet what God does with it is big.

Jesus' parables remind me of the attitude of Brother Lawrence in his book, *The Practice of the Presence of God*. It is said that because he was unable to do bigger things for God, he concentrated on doing little things.

How could that same attitude change the ordinary and seemingly mundane minutes and hours of your day? How could that impact your relationship with your neighbors? A boss or your friends? Let's do what Jesus calls us to do—little things. Small things. With great love and humility. Those are big things in God's eyes!

POINTS TO PONDER

What ordinary tasks is God calling you to see as small acts of love?

_____

_____

_____

It's not what we do; it's how we do what we do. Even small things can be big things when done in love toward God and others. Write down the names of a few people you can do something small for today.

_____

_____

_____

PAUSING TO PRAY

Father, as an offering of love, I give you the small tasks of _____

_____

56 | Gazing Ahead, Not Glancing Behind

Karen

Scripture to Study

Say not, "Why were the former days better than these?"
For it is not from wisdom that you ask this.

Ecclesiastes 7:10 ESV

When my teenagers created my very first social media account for me, I was a bit reluctant, thinking it was more for kids than adults. But after a while, I learned to navigate the various sites and was soon posting and commenting with the best of them.

A few of the sites include a feature that sends memories to you unsolicited that suddenly appear on your screen. These are posts from the past, usually something I put on my account one, five, or even ten years ago. Unfortunately, these flashes from the past sometimes deflate my spirit.

One morning I was greeted with a five-year-old memory of my mom, my daughter, and me on our yearly three-generational Christmas shopping excursion. Since we'd just buried my mom a few months prior, seeing that image inflated my heart with fresh grief, knowing we'd never get to sip peppermint mochas while searching for holiday gifts again.

Another time, a post popped up from when my now-grown children were all still in school. It was of myself along with several other baseball moms at an out-of-state weekend tournament. While it made me smile to think back on the days I'd spent parked in a lawn chair and cheering on the blue and orange Grand Rapids Flames, the nostalgia also made my heart sink, knowing my days as a sports mom were over.

The very contemplative book of Ecclesiastes warns us about the practice of wishing we still dwelt in the past. Ecclesiastes 7:10 chides, "Say not, 'Why were the former days better than these?' For it is not from wisdom that you ask this." Perhaps the writer of this book—thought by most Christian and Jewish scholars to be King Solomon—warns not to look back because doing so often prevents us from moving forward.

Keeping our eyes riveted on the past can also indicate an attitude of ungratefulness for all that we have in the present. When I find myself longing for the former days, I know I need to funnel my thoughts to thankfulness, going so far as to thank God for the things that are no longer, the things I so desperately miss. Let me explain.

The loss of loved ones still led to good because others came to faith in Christ due to the testimony of the now-deceased person. A change in the activities of my kids as they grow might make me sorrowful, but it also frees up more time for ministry. When I purpose to seek out glimmers of good, I often unearth them buried just beneath the layers of loss.

Let's decide together that we will stop longing for the former days and instead look all around at the blessings and provisions God has for us today. It's time we stopped glancing behind and started gazing ahead.

POINTS TO PONDER

Identify a memory from your past that makes you sad because things have changed.

_____

_____

How might today's Scripture help you think differently about this situation?

_____

_____

_____

Creator of time, *help me to stop longing for the former days. I decide today that I will begin to* _____

_____

_____

_____

_____

_____

57 | Envy Rots the Bones

Ruth

Scripture to Study

And I saw that all toil and all achievement spring from one person's envy of another. This too is meaningless, a chasing after the wind.

Ecclesiastes 4:4

I remember one time, almost seventeen years ago, when my husband and I went to visit his parents, who were living in Fort Wayne, Indiana. They had a huge chest freezer in the basement—the kind you load full of ice cream, frozen pizzas, vegetables, meat, and anything else you want to keep frozen in the event of a food crisis!

On the first night of our stay, we made a horrible discovery. It wasn't a food shortage—it was the freezer. The freezer had lost power, and nobody knew for how long. But when we opened the lid, it became obvious to everyone in the house that it had stopped working a long time ago. There is no way for me to describe the horrific smell! Yes, it was that awful.

There was melted ice cream. Rotten meat. Moldy vegetables. The smell of death immediately penetrated and permeated the entire house! It was horrible. As I think back to that unfortunate event, I can't help but think of what the Bible has to say about envy.

"A heart at peace gives life to the body, but envy rots the bones" (Proverbs 14:30). Or the writer of Ecclesiastes says it this way: "And I saw that all toil and all achievement spring from one person's envy of another. This too is meaningless, a chasing after the wind" (4:4).

In other words, envy, the sorrow over someone else's success, "rots the bones." While jealousy is seeking to protect what is ours, envy is wanting what is someone else's. Envy is like that rotten freezer. It is the perfect environment for breeding all sorts of dead and rotting stuff like anger, resentment, suspicion, competition, flattery, and lies.

We spend so much time and energy focusing on others; we desire to possess what they possess. So we "toil" to get what they have. Yet it never truly satisfies. It rots our bones and it is "meaningless." Those are harsh words, but it is important to understand the seriousness of envy in the Bible.

It's easy to get caught up in comparing our life with someone else's, isn't it? We see someone else's vacation. Someone else's family. Someone else's ministry. Someone else's health or job or marriage. You get the point, because you, like me, have felt the pain of someone else's success!

But what God wants for us is not death, it is life. He wants, as the Scripture says, a healthy heart. And that is a "heart at peace." That kind of heart is one that gives life and not death to the body. It has an aroma of joy and gratitude and humility.

POINTS TO PONDER

How would you describe the condition of your heart as it relates to envy?

_____

_____

Gratitude guards our hearts against envy. When we focus on what we don't have, we become sorrowful. When we focus on what we do have, we grow more grateful. Why is it sometimes a struggle to focus on the good things God has provided for you?

_____

_____

PAUSING TO PRAY

Father, give me grace to be grateful for what I have and don't deserve. Thank you for _____

58 | Great Expectations

Karen

Scripture to Study

The LORD is good to all,
And His tender mercies are over all His works.

Psalm 145:9 NKJV

In almost every season of life, there are situations lurking on the horizon about which we aren't exactly sure just what we can expect.

When I was a teenager, I often thought about what life would be like after high school. I knew I wanted to go to college, but I wasn't sure if my single mom would be able to financially swing it. I also pondered what my future would bring as far as a career; my interests were all over the map. I toggled between wanting to be a pharmacist, a television news reporter, or a high school history teacher.

Once I was in college, my thoughts turned to life after graduation. Would I stay in the Midwest? Move to another area of the country? Would I be traversing life solo, or would a man come along who would someday be my husband? And then, once I was married, I wondered about things like children and moves, aging parents and forging lifetime friendships. There have also been concerning times of financial stress and medical test results.

Throughout all of it—although in my heart and mind I knew God was in control—something within me wanted to know exactly what I could expect next. Ever the planner and color-coded schedule-maker, I yearned to know the steps that lay ahead long before I ever needed to take them.

Looking back now at over four decades of life, I can see that sometimes things turned out much as I expected. Other times, the exact opposite occurred. Things I'd vowed would never happen—like being a June bride and having three kids (I wanted to avoid the dreaded stereotypical "oldest, middle, youngest child" syndrome)—were exactly what *did* transpire. But here is the one thing that I can say was consistent: God always planned good for me, even though there were instances in which I didn't realize it at the time. Later on—peering in hindsight— these situations made sense.

Psalm 145:9 asserts, "The LORD is good to all, and His tender mercies are over all His works." I just love the definition of the Hebrew word *racham*, translated in this verse as *tender mercies*. *Racham* means foremost having a deep and intense compassion and showing infinite and absolute love. And when we read that "the LORD is good to all," guess what the word *all* is in the Hebrew? *Kol*, and it means all. All means all! And that includes you.

At those times when we don't know what to expect from life, the one great expectation we can surely possess is that God is full of tender mercy. His compassion is deep, his kindness, intense. In his wisdom he allows our life situations to materialize only after being run through a grid of his infinite and absolute love for us.

What can you and I expect in the future? Neither of us knows. But we *can* know with certainty that the Lord is good. He is good to us. His mercies won't ever come to an end (Lamentations 3:22).

▎POINTS TO PONDER ▶

What situation(s) are you now concerned about because you are not sure what to expect?

How can the explanation of the phrase *tender mercies* help to calm your heart about this issue?

_____

_____

_____

_____

_____

PAUSING TO PRAY

Merciful Lord, even though I do not know what to expect in the future, I do know that you _____

_____

_____

_____

59 | Stressed and Looking for Rest

Ruth

Scripture to Study

Truly my soul finds rest in God; my salvation comes from him.

Psalm 62:1

"How are you comforting yourself?" a friend asked me. "What are you doing with your pain?" To be honest, I hadn't given my hurt that much thought. I was just trying to get through. I was trying to gut it out.

But she was right—stress and sorrow and hurt always come with a choice: What will we do with our hurt? How will we choose to comfort ourselves?

In verse 3 of Psalm 62, the psalmist cries out in his distress, "how long," indicating that this is not a new set of circumstances. He's been in a bad place for some time. And he likens himself to a "leaning wall, this tottering fence." In other words, he's weak and worn out and it wouldn't take much for him to just buckle under the stress of it all!

You know the feeling. You have felt the weight. You've been in the tunnel—the dark one with no light in sight. We've probably all flinched from the fatigue. We weep. We wait. And we wonder if or when God is going to come through.

There is a common pattern we see in the psalms of lament, these psalms that are expressions of our sorrow and questions and hurt. We see a complaint and then a petition, but then always some kind of declaration of trust or hope or faithfulness. A defiant resolution.

I love the reminder in the opening verse of this psalm, about where we must always take our pain. "Truly my soul finds rest in God; my salvation comes from him."

"Salvation," or help, comes from God. He alone is the One who puts our soul at rest. The psalmist uses the Hebrew word *dumiyyah* for rest, which means to be quiet or still in waiting. Of all the places we can take our stress, only God puts our soul at ease!

Friend, I know it is tempting to turn to someone else or something else in our waiting and wondering. But only God can help us wait patiently and trust confidently. Only God can give us the strength that sustains us and enables us to say as the psalmist did, "I will never be shaken" (Psalm 62:2).

POINTS TO PONDER

What does it look like to comfort yourself in godly ways?

_____

_____

_____

Suffering comes with a choice. In the middle of your chaos, God wants you to lean on him. How can understanding the rest God offers change the way we suffer?

_____

_____

_____

PAUSING TO PRAY

Father, still my soul. Help me to not be shaken in this season of

_____

_____

60 | Thank You for Being a Friend

Karen

Scripture to Study

I thank my God in all my remembrance of you.

Philippians 1:3 ESV

Each Christmas break, after the tree and other shimmery yuletide decorations had been taken down, my mom insisted I write thank-you notes to the family and friends who'd sent me gifts. Writing these letters of gratitude—carefully, in my very best cursive—gave way to a love of writing notes of gratitude still today.

In the apostle Paul's letter to the church at Philippi, we see a thank-you of sorts—his immense gratefulness for his friends. He wasn't writing this letter to just new acquaintances, but mostly to dear friends, having founded the church a decade prior. He refers to their relationship as a "partnership in the gospel" (Philippians 1:5). This partnership wasn't just a loose association or a casual emotional connection. The original language had physical and financial overtones, meaning they'd taken care of each other's basic needs, sharing money and goods in addition to sharing encouragement.

The apostle was confident of the hope his friends had in Christ, sharing his certainty that God, who had begun a good work, would continue to move in their lives, bringing it to completion in Jesus Christ (Philippians 1:6). Paul was confident God was working in his friends' lives. He didn't give in to despair about their life decisions, which we sometimes do, but instead prayed for his fellow believers and placed them in God's hands.

The words for *began* and *completion* in Philippians 1:6 are the same words that refer to the beginning and end of a Greek sacrifice. The life of every Christian is a sacrifice ready to be offered to Jesus Christ for the sake of the gospel. Elsewhere in Scripture, Paul used similar imagery when he urged believers to present their bodies as a living sacrifice (Romans 12:1). Part of our life of sacrifice is our interactions with others, for the sake of the gospel.

Because he had received God's grace, Paul could share it freely with others. Sharing God's grace prevents our hearts from becoming gripped with envy. This could have happened since Paul was in prison when others were free. And yet we sense Paul loved these people with the affection of Jesus rather than simple human love.

This supernatural affection allowed their bonds to be strong and to weather the storms that sometimes come along in relationships. Loving our friends with the affection of Jesus will allow us to be truly thankful for all our interactions with them—even the difficult times. Loving each other, offering forgiveness when wronged, and then forging ahead in our friendships displays the gospel to a watching world.

Can we adopt a grateful mindset as well—expressing thankfulness to our friends who help us emotionally and physically in our times of need? It not only blesses them, but gratitude for others helps to grow our faith.

Is there someone you thank God for every time they come to mind? Reach out to them today to tell them how grateful you are for their friendship.

POINTS TO PONDER

Is there a fellow Christian who—when you remember them—causes you to burst with gratitude to God?

What specifically about them or their actions toward you makes you most thankful?

_____

_____

_____

PAUSING TO PRAY

Father God, thank you for my Christian friends. May I love them by _____

_____

_____

_____

_____

_____

61 | Waiting

Ruth

Scripture to Study

When the people saw that Moses was so long in coming down from the mountain, they gathered around Aaron and said, "Come, make us gods who will go before us. As for this fellow Moses who brought us up out of Egypt, we don't know what has happened to him."

Exodus 32:1

We all know what it is like to wait. The Israelites were no exception. In fact, their waiting, in the wrong way, was so important that even the New Testament records it as a warning to us today (1 Corinthians 10:6–7).

Not only *what* we are waiting on, but *how* we wait, matters. And our waiting often reveals what is going on in our hearts. Our waiting reveals our faith.

Exodus 32 records that familiar story of the Israelites getting impatient when it seemed like Moses was taking too long on the mountain with God. Instead of trusting God, they turned and made a false god, an idol—a golden calf.

The Israelites didn't want to trust God; they wanted a tangible god. They wanted something they could see. The sin of their idolatry was really a refusal to walk by faith. But what is most surprising about their waiting? The very reason God's people were waiting is because Moses was receiving from the Lord plans for building a tabernacle!

In other words, here are the Israelites getting antsy waiting on God, yet little do they know why it's taking so long. Little do they know what he is doing—what he is preparing! The Creator God who shaped the heavens was making plans to come dwell with his people in a new way.

The Covenant-Keeping God who delivered them out of Egypt was about to draw near to be among his people!

So what does all of this mean for us today? It means that in our waiting, God is often preparing something better for us. He is doing something we do not yet see. And he is wanting to purify our desires and our dreams so that in our waiting, what we want most is to do God's will.

◗ POINTS TO PONDER

How would you describe your waiting?

_____

_____

_____

Waiting purifies our will. Jesus taught us to pray for God's will to be done on earth as it is in heaven (Matthew 6:10). And he modeled for us what it looks like to say, "Not my will, but yours be done" (Luke 22:42). Why do you think it can be so hard for us to wait?

_____

_____

_____

_____

PAUSING TO PRAY

Father, *I want what you want. I will trust you with* _____

_____

_____

62 | Unexpected, but Perfect, Pairings

Karen

Scripture to Study

Rejoice in hope; be patient in affliction; be persistent in prayer.

Romans 12:12 csb

I'm always pleasantly surprised when two things I think surely don't belong together turn out to instead be a delight, like the sea salt and caramel latte I ordered last week. My father used to sprinkle pepper on his cantaloupe. I thought this pairing rather bizarre, and I liked my cantaloupe quite plain, thank you very much. But when I decided to be brave one day and try it, I found out it was indeed delicious.

At first glance, Romans 12:12 appears to tether to each other some words and concepts that don't naturally seem to belong together. The first pairing is comprised of *rejoicing* and *hope*.

I can't think about the concept of hope without thoughts of uncertainty also showing up on the scene. If I am hoping something turns out to be true, it means that I have no guarantees it will. In fact, I'm often *doubting* that it will. And so, being told in this passage to simultaneously rejoice while I am hoping? Well, it kind of seems foreign to me. I'm not always joyful over things I can't control. On the contrary, having to wonder sometimes siphons the joy right out of my life.

The next line we see drawn connects patience to affliction. Say what? When I am being afflicted, patience has left the building. I'm strategizing how I might escape from the pain, and I want to concoct a plan pronto! I can't seem to take my mind off my troubles. The concept of patience

164

evokes images of dire durations. Affliction is not something I want to book a long and leisurely visit with.

Finally, we see persistence hitched to the practice of prayer. If something is a serious matter of prayer in my life, I'd prefer that the answer to that prayer come about sooner rather than later. Persistence to me sounds so long-term and quite draining—like I'm going to need to keep showing up and hanging in there. Just thinking about summoning some stick-to-it persistence in my behavior makes my brain tired.

Over the years, with each of these pairings, God has slowly shown me that I was looking at them all wrong. I need to not look at what trying to display joy-filled hope, to acquire patience when afflicted, or to show persistence in prayer might get *for* me but rather understand what these actions can do *in* me.

Having joy while dwelling in the uncertainty of now can showcase to others our trust in God. Patience during affliction develops in us faith and empathy, and positions us to offer encouragement to others who are also afflicted. And finally, persistence in prayer teaches us how to more fully trust God and takes our relationship with him to a much deeper level than just rattling off a list of "give me" and "bless them" snippets of prayer.

Can we welcome the situation of uncertainty that teaches us to choose joy? Can we embrace the unwanted afflictions that bring to us the wanted characteristic of patience? And will the prayers of our hearts make us persist, helping to mold us to be more like Christ?

In hope: joyful. In affliction: patient. In prayer: persistent. May welcoming these unexpected pairings become our aim.

POINT TO PONDER

Which of the three phrases in Romans 12:12 do you find most difficult and why?

PAUSING TO PRAY

Heavenly Father, *I long for you to develop in me* _____

_____

_____

_____

_____

_____

_____

63 | When Saying No Is Our Best Answer

Ruth

Scripture to Study

And when they found him, they exclaimed: "Everyone is looking for you!" Jesus replied, "Let us go somewhere else—to the nearby villages—so I can preach there also. That is why I have come."

Mark 1:37–38

felt the text message from a close friend at almost the same time I *read* it. As quickly as my eyes scanned it, my mind was processing it. But so was my body. I immediately felt the tension squeezing my neck and my heart rate accelerating.

It was another one of those text messages—you know, the kind that doesn't come out directly and say it but is meant to make you feel guilty? Guilty for saying "I can't" or, "Not right now." Guilty for considering any other option but "Yes!"

It wasn't a huge request. It was just that I didn't have anything left to give. Maybe it was a bad day. Or a reaction from the tough season we were in. I was dry, pulled in a million different directions, and now, disappointing a friend! Either way, it got me thinking. My mind and weary soul were drawn to the story of Jesus. Drawn to the example of the high demand on his life. Drawn to the way he knew how to get alone with the Father, which got him away from people who needed him.

When the disciples found him, early one morning after a long day of ministry, they couldn't help but blurt out, "Everyone is looking for you!" (Mark 1:37). Now, to be fair (or accurate), Jesus was not burned out. He wasn't hiding. He was disengaging from the needs of others to be nourished by his Father.

But what strikes me is that his response wasn't to meet every need; it was to move on. It was to say no. To say yes would have been a distraction. Mark records this in verse 38 by giving us Jesus' reaction: "Let us go somewhere else—to the nearby villages—so I can preach there also. That is why I have come." He continued on in what he was called to do.

It's okay not to be able to do everything for everyone. Boundaries keep us together. They keep us fueled. And focused on what matters most. If even Jesus needed to say no, how much more do we?

POINTS TO PONDER

Why do you think it is so difficult to say no to the requests of others?

_____

_____

Saying no is often necessary to enable us to stay rooted in Christ and what he has called us to do. The needs around us and our responsibility to them change in each season. Who are the people and what are the circumstances you need to say no to? What will your no enable you to say yes to?

_____

_____

_____

PAUSING TO PRAY

Father, give me wisdom to say yes to what I need to by saying no to _____

64 | Why Do a Good Deed?

Karen

Scripture to Study

For we are God's handiwork, created in Christ Jesus to do good works, which God prepared in advance for us to do.

Ephesians 2:10

Lately I've had fun observing a chain of kind deeds on our little town's Facebook page. It all started when someone hopped on the page to post a thank-you to the person who paid for her coffee that morning at the local fast-food drive-thru. She said she decided to continue the chain of thoughtfulness by paying for the person's meal behind her. Many residents hopped on to say how considerate these actions were and that they too were challenged to do something similar.

The simple gesture of a gifted latte sparked a flurry of good deeds. In the weeks following, people took to the comments thread to thank those who'd helped them in various ways.

An elderly woman expressed her gratitude for having her heavy groceries carried to her car on a rainy afternoon. A young mom thanked a stranger for helping her fold her stroller at the park when she had her hands full with a crying baby and a wriggling toddler. Still another man expressed his astonishment when he discovered his breakfast had been paid for at our local diner by another patron.

When it comes to kind deeds, some religions tout a "good works" mentality, teaching that if we do enough good in the world, God will allow us into heaven. But as believers in Jesus, we know that we are not saved by anything we can do, good works included.

In the original Greek, the word *good* in Ephesians 2:10 is *agathos*. It means that something is intrinsically kind. It is a true goodness that originates from God and is empowered by him. We don't perform these works in our own strength. We do them through the Lord's strength instead.

The term for *kind* in the definition of *agathos* above is an adjective in the Greek—*chréstos*. It is a combination of two concepts—kind and useful. There isn't an English word that, when used by itself, conveys the dual meaning here. *Chréstos* means both earthly thoughtful and eternally useful. It serves a purpose. This divine benevolence is beneficial because it may lead others to repentance. Yes. Your kindness to others, which flows from God himself, can be a conduit to show them God's kindness, which may in turn spark a desire in them to follow him too.

It is God's kindness—not his condemnation—that wins others to himself (Romans 2:4). And our kindness when doing good deeds can help to win others over as well.

Today, let's be open to how God can prompt our kindness and do some of the good works he has already prepared for us to do. Just remember that good works aren't our ticket to heaven . . . they are our marching orders here on earth.

POINTS TO PONDER

How does it make you feel, knowing that God has already prepared good works for you here on earth?

_____

_____

How might you be more intentional in carrying through with performing them to point people to Christ?

_____

_____

_____

PAUSING TO PRAY

Father, *may my kindness to others originate from you and be empowered by your Holy Spirit. Help my behavior to* _____

_____

_____

_____

_____

_____

65 | Worry's Prediction

Ruth

Worry most often lives in tomorrow. Anxiety anticipates. It zooms in on all of the possibilities of what could happen. And most often, it predicts not the presence of God, but his absence. After all, if we really believe God would be present, what would there be to fear?

The apostle Paul was no stranger to hardship. He knew trials. It seems as if danger was always awaiting him. He knew physical pain, spiritual rejection, financial insecurity, and certainly a lot more. So what he tells us in 2 Corinthians 12:9 is insightful as we set our gaze on all that could go wrong in a fallen world!

After describing his own weakness, this mysterious "thorn" he was given, he draws our attention not to his weaknesses or to the what-ifs, but to the grace of God. He wants to settle us with the sustaining presence and power of God. He writes, "But he said to me, 'My grace is sufficient for you, for my power is made perfect in weakness.' Therefore I will boast all the more gladly about my weaknesses, so that Christ's power may rest on me."

God's grace is enough—it is sufficient. Whatever weakness you may face, the one that keeps you up at night or the one that is nagging you right now . . . whatever possibility scares you . . . whatever situation or circumstance may steal your power, there is a great power that does and will rest on you.

Here is one of the ways God's grace is a solution to our worry. You know that prediction you are making about the future? God gives us the grace when we need it. So do not worry, my friend! Even if it does come true, God's grace will be enough for you to endure. You'll make it. Not because you are strong, but because God is present. His power, present in his grace, will be enough in your weakness!

POINTS TO PONDER

In what area(s) of your life do you need the reminder of the sufficiency of God's grace?

_____

_____

_____

While God does not promise us a future without pain or loss, he does promise us a future in which he is present and powerful enough to sustain us. How will you freely walk in that promise today?

_____

_____

_____

_____

PAUSING TO PRAY

Father, *give me grace to endure* _____

_____

66 | Putting Life in Portrait Mode

Karen

Scripture to Study

But one thing I do: Forgetting what is behind and reaching forward to what is ahead, I pursue as my goal the prize promised by God's heavenly call in Christ Jesus.

Philippians 3:13–14 CSB

I often have trouble focusing. Not my eyes, but my mind. My thoughts love to wander. They trip me up, reminding me of a past mistake, habitual weakness, or possible future scenario that might go horribly wrong. No matter how I try to boss my brain around, I can't seem to make it concentrate. My phone, however, has a great feature for bringing focus.

Recently, while snapping a picture on my phone of my budding bubble-gum-pink geraniums, I used a camera element called portrait mode. This feature makes the main subject of a photograph stay in focus while the rest of the background blurs. My geraniums seemed to leap off the screen, becoming the clear center of attention when up against the haziness of the rest of the backyard. If only our brains came equipped with a portrait mode!

As we navigate our days, sometimes our past mistakes, wrong choices, or long-held habits threaten to steal our attention away from what we should be focusing on—what matters most.

Philippians 3:13–14 gives us encouragement and direction as to where our attention should lie. The apostle Paul states that he does one thing: forgets what is behind and reaches forward to what is ahead.

Paul is referring to athletes who run a race, emphasizing the importance of keeping one's eyes looking forward, not turning to glance behind. Looking back would slow the runner, causing a loss of focus on the path ahead. However, when Paul fixes his gaze forward, he isn't tripped up but pursues as his goal, "the prize promised by God's heavenly call in Christ Jesus."

The image is even more powerful when we study the meaning of the Greek word translated as "forgetting." The word in its original form doesn't mean merely a failure to remember—such as when you forget a medical appointment in a brain blip. It means calculated and purposeful neglect, a realization that you no longer care. This intentional abandonment encompasses forgetting things, events, times, and places.

This deliberate ignoring of the past permits Paul to run unimpeded and with clear focus toward the goal. What is this goal he is racing toward? It signifies an end-marker of a footrace. Paul is using it to mark the end of our race of faith in this earthly life.

Will you fix your gaze ahead today rather than letting the past distract you from where God would have you go? When we purpose to focus solely on Jesus, the past fades, distractions blur, and we find our faith renewed. We are free to follow God wherever he is leading us.

POINTS TO PONDER

What past mistakes, wrong choices, or long-held habits threaten to overtake your thoughts?

_____

_____

_____

_____

_____

_____

_____

How might you use Paul's example of forgetting what lies behind to implement a calculated and purposeful neglect of this distraction?

_____

_____

_____

_____

_____

Father, _please help me fix my gaze forward, riveting my eyes only upon you. May the past _____

_____

_____

_____

67 | The Blindness of Comparison

Ruth

Scripture to Study

Don't I have the right to do what I want with my own money? Or are you envious because I am generous?

Matthew 20:15

Who are those friends who are quick to celebrate with you and for you? Your happiness is their happiness. Your success is theirs. And your win is a win for them too. My guess, those friends or family members are few and far between!

Why is it so hard for others to celebrate with us? Or, turning the question toward our own hearts, why is it so hard for us, for me, to celebrate when others succeed or experience the goodness of God?

If I look at my own heart, I am increasingly made aware of how self-focused my heart it is. Okay, let me put it even more bluntly—how prideful and ungrateful I can be. I begin comparing what I have with what others have been given, failing to celebrate with and for those I am called to love most!

Comparison robs us of the ability to celebrate the goodness of God in the lives of those around us.

This is a point Jesus makes in his parable of the landowners in Matthew 20:1–16. He tells the story of a landowner who goes out to hire people to work in his vineyard. He goes out early in the morning and hires some laborers. Then he goes again at 9 a.m., noon, three in the afternoon, and finally at 5 p.m. Here comes the surprising part—and the conviction!

When it came time for each to receive their paycheck, those who were hired first were expecting to be paid a lot more. After all, they had been working longer. But instead, the landowner pays each worker the same. At this, those who were hired first, those who thought they deserved more, began to grumble. The landowner then responds by saying, "Don't I have the right to do what I want with my own money? Or are you envious because I am generous?" (Matthew 20:15).

The workers' comparison led to envy. Their envy blinded them, preventing them from being grateful for what they did receive and did not deserve. This led to their inability to celebrate the grace of God in the lives of the other workers!

Let's have our hearts moved and molded by God's grace. Let's not compare ourselves with others; let's celebrate with others. After all, we have all been given more than we deserve!

POINTS TO PONDER

How can you compare less and celebrate more?

_____

_____

Envy always robs us of our gratitude and joy. It always wants more and grieves when others have more than we think we have. When we stop comparing, we'll start celebrating! Take a few minutes to send a text to a few people you can encourage and celebrate with today.

_____

_____

_____

PAUSING TO PRAY

Father, enable me to have a heart that celebrates others. Forgive me, for I have been envious by _____

68 | Cultivated, Not Just Imitated

Karen

Scripture to Study

When they observed the boldness of Peter and John and realized that they were uneducated and untrained men, they were amazed and recognized that they had been with Jesus.

Acts 4:13 CSB

When our oldest son, Mitchell, was a tiny tot, we purchased a toy lawn mower for him at a local yard sale. Using that plaything became one of his favorite pastimes. But he didn't want to propel it just anywhere. He wanted to follow along right behind his dad as he mowed the lawn. Of course, this wasn't very safe since the lawn mower blade might throw a rock or other object. So my husband disengaged the mower blade and pushed his lawn mower around our backyard just so my son could follow behind and imitate him.

While Mitch did love mimicking his dad, that wasn't the main point of his play. He just constantly wanted to be where his father was. Whether my husband was outside in the yard, working on something in the garage, or putting his feet up inside the house after finishing his chores, our son stuck close by his side, loving the time spent in his presence.

Often over the decades of my spiritual life, I thought that a worthy goal was to try to be more like Jesus, to imitate his behavior and behave like he did. But the older I get, the more I have discovered it isn't enough just to try to be *like* Jesus. Even more important, we should want to be *with* Jesus. Godly behavior can't just be imitated; it needs to be cultivated. And the best way to cultivate it is by spending time and effort to grow our relationship with the Lord.

179

A certain phrase pops out at me from Acts 4:13. When people observed Peter and John being bold, despite being uneducated and untrained men, Scripture tells us "they were amazed and recognized that they had been with Jesus."

How this half sentence tagged on to the end of the verse can both challenge and inspire us! Do others recognize from our behavior that we have been with Jesus? Might they be amazed at qualities we possess, even though we aren't anybody special? In our walk with the King, are we focusing less on copying his behavior in a perfunctory way and more on just being in his presence, allowing the Holy Spirit to convict, change, and embolden us, helping us trust God more and live out our faith?

First Chronicles 16:11 states, "Seek the LORD and His strength; Seek His face continually [longing to be in His presence]" (AMP). Do you long to be in God's presence? Do you make it a high priority in life? Spending deliberate and concerted time with Jesus—however that works into your schedule and season—shows a seriousness about our faith and can strengthen our trust in him.

Let the words of James 4:8 be your continual ambition: "Come close to God, and God will come close to you" (NLT). Don't try too hard to replicate the Lord's behavior. Looking and sounding like him will be the natural result from spending time with him so often. Focus on that instead.

POINTS TO PONDER

Do you need to make any changes in how seriously, or how often, you spend concentrated time in God's presence?

What changes do you desire to see?

_____

_____

_____

_____

PAUSING TO PRAY

Gracious Father, *I long to put spending unhurried time with you at the top of my priority list. This week I will* _____

_____

_____

_____

_____

_____

_____

69 | What Time Is It?

Ruth

Scripture to Study

From that time on Jesus began to explain to his disciples that he must go to Jerusalem and suffer many things at the hands of the elders, the chief priests and the teachers of the law, and that he must be killed and on the third day be raised to life.

Matthew 16:21

We had been driving for maybe thirty minutes when our youngest daughter, Sophia, inquired, "What time is it?" We had only logged thirty minutes of a nine-hour drive! And already she and our other kids were wondering how much longer!

Of course, you don't have to be a parent to know what it's like to pay attention to time—to be aware of how much, or how little, time we may have.

Kids are not the only ones who pay attention to time. When we look at the life of Jesus, we notice that he was always aware of what time it was. It was his awareness of time that enabled him to act in time, wisely and effectively.

One example we see of this is in Matthew 16:21. Most Bible commentators point out that this verse is a turning point in Matthew's gospel. It marks a significant transition due to Jesus' sense of time.

From that time on Jesus began to explain to his disciples that he must go to Jerusalem and suffer many things at the hands of the elders, the chief priests and the teachers of the law, and that he must be killed and on the third day be raised to life.

Verse 21 starts out, "From that time on . . ." Matthew is telling us that Jesus knew exactly what time it was! It was time for him to begin telling his disciples about what awaited him in Jerusalem—his death and resurrection. Jesus' sense of time moved him to act and teach and invest differently. He knew the season and the circumstances he was in.

What time is it for *you*? What is Jesus calling you to do, or not do, in this season or set of circumstances?

POINTS TO PONDER

For the season you are in, how would you finish the sentence "From this time on . . ."?

_____

_____

_____

_____

_____

Our awareness of time enables us to act more wisely in time. As you think about the season or circumstances you are currently in, take some time to prayerfully ask Jesus for insight on how to live most effectively for him.

PAUSING TO PRAY

Father, show me what you want from me right now. From this time on, *help me to* _____

_____

_____

70 | Be on the Lookout

Karen

Scripture to Study

For thus the Lord said to me: "Go, set a watchman; let him announce what he sees."

Isaiah 21:6 ESV

When I was in elementary school, we neighborhood kids often played outside together. Usually it was kickball or hide-and-seek, but sometimes the girls would use a picnic table, some lawn chairs, and a few blankets to erect a makeshift fort. There we'd hide out from the boys, eating snacks and sharing secrets. We'd take turns having one girl crouch in the tall grass of a nearby vacant field to be on the lookout for any approaching boys who might threaten to crash our private party.

In Isaiah 21, we see the Lord instructing the prophet Isaiah, "Go, set a watchman; let him announce what he sees" This watchman's duty was to describe the attacking foes, particularly the countless cavalrymen approaching on assorted four-legged creatures.

The scout would wait for days and nights and then give his account. This was taking place in the wilderness of ancient Babylon, most likely the portion of land bordering the Persian Gulf. This land was a vast, flat, swampy marshland overflowed by both the Tigris and Euphrates rivers. It was prophesied to be destroyed by giant whirlwinds coming from the wilderness. In this region there were often storms that descended upon Judea, coming from the south and triggering serious destruction.

The prophet announced the approaching fall of Babylon and its idolatrous inhabitants by crying out (Isaiah 21:8). The Hebrew language here suggests this cry as a lion-like roar. However, it is not to be feared by the people, for the proclamation was enveloped in a message of comfort for the nation of Israel. The image given in Isaiah 21:10 of being threshed and winnowed is commonly employed by Old Testament poets to paint a picture of the powerful punishment of the wicked that is coupled with the refining trials of the righteous.

Are there storms beginning to brew on the horizon of your life? Do you fear your finances may fail or that you—or a loved one—may experience physical distress? Or perhaps you are currently walking through a relational battle that is taking its toll on your heart and occupying your mind. These potential situations can cause an unsettling in our souls. However, they can also drive us to look to Jesus.

As believers today, we need not fear any coming trial or atmospheric storms. We can trust that our God is in control as we, like a diligent watchman, rivet our eyes on our Creator and his Word while the future unfolds here on earth. Then, one day the Lion of Judah—our Lord and Savior, Jesus Christ—will return to defeat every foe and gain the final victory (Revelation 5:5). Until then, we keep watching, keep trusting, keeping taking God at his Word, knowing he won't ever abandon his own (Deuteronomy 31:8).

POINT TO PONDER

When you think of the future return of the Lion of Judah, how should this affect your thoughts and actions as you live your life in the present?

_____

_____

_____

PAUSING TO PRAY

Father God, thank you for the diligent way you watch over all of history, rewarding good and punishing evil. I'm so grateful that

_____

71 | Seek First

Ruth

Scripture to Study

But seek first his kingdom and his righteousness, and all these things will be given to you as well. Therefore do not worry about tomorrow, for tomorrow will worry about itself. Each day has enough trouble of its own.

Matthew 6:33–34

I realized recently how often I use the word *first*. Our youngest daughter, Sophia, recently asked me to check her Instagram on my phone. "Yes, of course," I responded, "but *first* let me finish this email." My youngest son, Noah, asked a similar question about playing a video game. "Make sure your room is clean *first*!" I find myself saying this often because when the more pressing priorities are addressed first, things seem more in order, and I feel settled. I've found that isn't terribly different in my relationship with Jesus.

Seeking Jesus first, and putting him first, is what we are called to in the Christian life. And yet, as we all know, this is not easy or natural! Which is why we need the grace of God to grow. And to trust. But as we'll see, the fruit of putting Jesus first leads to a more settled, restful, worry-free life. Everything else fades when we put God first in everything.

This can be a struggle for me. So much of my coming to God in prayer is to get something from God. I'm guessing you feel the same. Maybe we want a new job. Better health. More money. Our list is long, and our longings aren't always bad. But what we need most is a relationship. That is what comes first. This is what Jesus is getting at in Matthew 6:33–34 when he uses the word *first*: "But seek first his kingdom and his righteousness, and all these things will be given to you as well. Therefore do not worry about tomorrow, for tomorrow will worry about itself. Each day has enough trouble of its own."

We are to seek God first. His kingdom and his way of life is to be the top priority and the top pursuit of our life. When we come to God, is his friendship enough for us? Is knowing and being known by him what truly satisfies? Trusting God in all the things begins with treasuring God above all other things!

POINTS TO PONDER

Where do you struggle to put God first in your life?

_____

_____

_____

What we need most is a deeper relationship with God the Father, through the Son, and in the power of the Holy Spirit. How can learning to put God first impact your spiritual life?

_____

_____

_____

_____

PAUSING TO PRAY

Father, I will seek you first by _____

_____

_____

72 | Breaking Free from Heartache and Hurt

Karen

> **Scripture to Study**
>
> Listen to my cry, for I am in desperate need; rescue me from those who pursue me, for they are too strong for me. Set me free from my prison, that I may praise your name. Then the righteous will gather about me because of your goodness to me.
>
> Psalm 142:6–7

The other day, one of my friends failed to use her blinker and got pulled over. The officer only gave her a warning, but he also gave her a troubling piece of information when he discovered she had inadvertently failed to renew her driver's license. An expired license could result in a $500 fine and up to ninety-three days in jail! (You can bet I set an alarm on my phone's calendar to remind me to renew my own license long before it will expire!)

While I haven't been incarcerated behind metal bars, I have been in prison. There have been a few seasons in my life when I have felt as if I were in an emotional prison because of other people's words or actions.

When I was a young girl, a family member's immoral actions tore away my sense of security and caused me to fear the future, placing me in a penitentiary of fear.

As a teen, the gossiping ways of a few former friends greatly affected my social standing, holding my confidence captive.

When I was an adult raising young children, some acquaintances pressured me to adopt their exact ways of behaving when it came to matters of faith. Their stringent practices smacked strongly of legalism (following rules just for the sake of following rules) and stifled any freedom I had to live out my faith in a biblical but different way. It flung me into a spiritual slammer.

As I walked through each of these seasons of emotional turmoil, I felt like a hostage. I just couldn't break free from the strong holds their words and actions had over me. The confinement hindered my happiness. The betrayal stung. The pressure brought anxiety. No matter what I did, I couldn't seem to break free from those hurts.

Psalm 142:6–7 is part of a prayer penned by the anointed but not-yet-king David as he was holed up in a cave, also longing to escape. He pleads to God, longing to be set free from his prison, that he might praise God's name.

David knew he could not escape his dire situation alone. His combined enemies' actions were just too strong. He needed God to rescue him. However, David didn't just long to break free for his own benefit. He found a greater purpose: praising God the Father in front of others, prompting them to gather and observe God's goodness.

During our seasons of emotional suffering, God can teach us to praise him despite our circumstances, positioning us to unearth the good in our grappling with the grief. When we go to him in desperation, longing to escape from what—or who—is incessantly pursuing us, he is faithful to break the chains and set us free, giving others a glimpse of his goodness.

Run to him now. He alone holds the keys to whatever is holding you captive.

POINTS TO PONDER

Describe a situation where you currently feel you're being held prisoner by other people's words or actions.

_____

_____

_____

How can you transform Psalm 142:6–7 into a personal prayer about this situation?

_____

_____

_____

_____

_____

_____

_____

_____

PAUSING TO PRAY

Father, at the times I feel trapped in an emotional prison, help me

_____

_____

_____

73 | No Regrets

Ruth

Scripture to Study

I have fought the good fight, I have finished the race, I have kept the faith.

2 Timothy 4:7

Does your past disturb you? Are there things you have done or said that not only still stick with you but at times cause you to be unsettled? We probably all live with some level of regret. There are things in each of our pasts that can haunt us today. Maybe things we've done that we shouldn't have. Or things we didn't do that we know we should have!

But here's the good news. A life without regret is possible. Rooting our life in God's love is the solution to a life lived with no regrets. The apostle Paul is a good example of this truth. Have you ever stopped to consider how remarkable his words are in 2 Timothy 4:7? Most scholars believe 2 Timothy is Paul's last letter, one he wrote not long before he died. And he wrote it to a much younger pastor, a spiritual son of Paul's named Timothy.

Paul comes to the end of his letter, likely knowing that the end of his life is near, and he writes, "I have fought the good fight, I have finished the race, I have kept the faith" (2 Timothy 4:7). Now remember, Paul's life was not exactly spotless! His past certainly had enough in it to disturb him. And yet, because of the love and forgiveness of God in Christ, Paul was able to look back on his life and say that he had run a good race. He was finishing well. He had kept the faith. He had no regrets!

How? Not because he didn't have a past, but because through repentance and faith, his past had been forgiven and redeemed. He had no regrets because his life was rooted in God's love. The cross was the cure. And as it was for Paul, so it can be for us!

If you are struggling with regret, remember God's grace. Give whatever it is over to the kindness and mercy of God in Christ. Repent where necessary. And then release it into the hands of Jesus. He died and rose again for you, to give you new life, freedom, and hope. He has covered your past with the cross. He doesn't want you to look back; Jesus wants you to look forward. Give him your past and he will give you a future, without regrets!

POINTS TO PONDER

What part of your past disturbs you most? Why?

_____

_____

_____

_____

When we give our past to God's love, he gives us a future without regrets. How can this truth change the way you live, starting today?

_____

_____

_____

_____

PAUSING TO PRAY

Father, I leave my past in your hands. Now give me the joy of a new future. I hand over to you _____

_____

74 | A Scriptural 9-1-1

Karen

Scripture to Study

Do not be far from me, my God;
come quickly, God, to help me.

Psalm 71:12

There have been a few times in my life when I rushed to dial 9-1-1. Twice as a witness to car accidents and once when I noticed a brush-fire burning wildly as I drove out in the countryside. In each instance, after describing the severe situation to the operator, I uttered something along the lines of, "Please hurry!" or "Come quickly!"

Psalm 70 is a short psalm that serves as a sort of Old Testament 9-1-1 plea for help. King David bookends the psalm with two similar supplications: "Hasten!" (v. 1) and "LORD, do not delay!" (v. 5). David seems to be begging the Lord not only to act but to please do it immediately!

This is not the first time in the book of Psalms that we encounter such an urgent petition. In fact, there are striking similarities between Psalm 70 and a portion of Psalm 40—specifically Psalm 40:13–17. Both passages use many of the same phrases and follow a nearly identical progression. It is quite possible that during the writing of Psalm 70, David intentionally referenced the verses in Psalm 40.

On the heels of this, Psalm 71 continues a theme of petitioning our Father in heaven due to a great need here on earth. There is no clear indication of who wrote Psalm 71, or when, but what is known to us is that the author penned the words when he was advancing in age and had acquired ample time over his life to ponder his long covenantal relationship with the living God.

The author had seen the Lord be a strong rock, ever ready to save (Psalm 71:3). He had been rescued by God from those who were wicked, unjust, and cruel (v. 4). However, he knew life was not over just yet, and he would still likely face trials, infirmities, and enemies until his dying day. Therefore, we observe the psalmist placing his hope continually in the Lord (v. 14) and even dialing up another spiritual 9-1-1 call, beseeching God to again make haste and save him in his time of trouble (Psalm 71:12).

These two psalms point to an important truth we can cling to in our own times of turmoil: The same God who showed up to rescue and save others in centuries past will still answer our own urgent calls of distress today.

- Are you worried or anxious? *Call on the Lord.*
- Do you fear what the future might bring? *Call on the Lord.*
- Are you walking through a relational storm? *Call on the Lord.*
- Do you look at your circumstances and long for someone to rescue you? *Call on the Lord.*

What a soothing assurance we have in knowing we can take all our worries and fears to God, trusting that he will hear and respond according to his perfect wisdom and will.

Call upon him, asking him to come quickly to your aid. He will answer every time.

POINTS TO PONDER

Can you recall a time when you had to offer up a spiritual 9-1-1 plea to God, such as the ones in today's reading?

_____

_____

_____

_____

How did the Lord intervene and rescue you—or someone you love—from a grim situation?

_____

_____

_____

_____

_____

_____

_____

_____

PAUSING TO PRAY

Father, *thank you for being the ultimate Responder to all the dilemmas I face. I praise you for* _____

_____

_____

_____

_____

75 | Getting Alone

Ruth

Scripture to Study

Very early in the morning, while it was still dark, Jesus got up, left the house and went off to a solitary place, where he prayed.

Mark 1:35

What does it really mean to be alone?

Getting alone is getting harder and harder in our culture. There is constant noise that surrounds us and it can feel like it is suffocating us. We can be tethered to a phone, bombarded with emails, or just worn out from legitimate needs or responsibilities.

As a result, we crave quiet. We long for alone time. Our soul is thirsty, whether we know it or not, for some rest. And yet this might surprise you, but solitude is relational.

Solitude is not about being alone with yourself; solitude is about being alone with God.

Being alone or on our own is what gets us in trouble! What we need most is to be with God. And regular times of silence and solitude allow us to do just that.

We get away from the internet. We leave our phones behind. We carve out space and time away from family or friends. And we focus on being with God. We read Scripture, pray, confess sin, and just sit quietly, listening for God's voice to speak to us.

This is the example we see in the life of Jesus. The Gospel of Mark records for us that after a busy day of ministry, Jesus got up early. Why? So he could get alone and get away. But again, not to be by himself, but to be with his Father. We read, "Very early in the morning, while it was

196

still dark, Jesus got up, left the house and went off to a solitary place, where he prayed" (Mark 1:35).

He got alone to listen to his Father's voice and to pray. He retreated from the normal demands and responsibilities of life and ministry. He lived out of the relationship he had with his Father and in the power of the Holy Spirit. This is the relationship that roots us. Anchors us.

Will you make room for him? With all of the noise, will you turn your ear and open your heart to his truth and love? Will you give him your attention so that Jesus will increasingly have your affection?

A life lived for God will flow out of a life deeply rooted in God.

POINTS TO PONDER

What are the biggest obstacles in your life right now that prevent solitude?

_____

_____

_____

What has our attention is usually what has our affection. Getting alone is about placing our hearts before Jesus and allowing him to speak to us, change us, and refuel us. Block out a time on your calendar this week when you will spend thirty minutes alone with him.

_____

_____

_____

PAUSING TO PRAY

Father, *I turn my attention back to you. I confess that I have given my affection to* _____

76 | Where Not to Place Your Trust

Karen

Scripture to Study

I will be the same until your old age,
and I will bear you up when you turn gray.
I have made you, and I will carry you;
I will bear and rescue you.

To whom will you compare me or make me equal?
Who will you measure me with,
so that we should be like each other?

Isaiah 46:4–5 CSB

My father recently passed away at the age of eighty-seven. For the last twenty or so years of his life, he and a handful of his buddies met for breakfast almost weekly. A friend joked that this group of guys should call themselves the ROMEO club—ROMEO standing for Retired Old Men Eating Out.

In all seriousness, I loved to hear my father tell stories of the steadfast presence of God in the lives of this band of brothers. Our heavenly Father, who had created each of them, had also carefully carried them throughout the many decades of their lives. He remained faithful until the very last one of them—my father—changed his address to heaven.

In Isaiah 46:4, we see this same steadfast love of God on display. However, it was not in God's faithfulness that the Babylonian people chose to place their trust. They turned instead to that which cannot save—idols. These idols were so weighty they had to be transported by huge animals. They were most likely forged from a precious metal such as gold or silver.

Throughout the Old Testament, we see warnings for those who futilely place their trust in false idols (Isaiah 42:17; 45:20; Habakkuk 2:18). But it isn't just the ancient Israelites in the Old Testament who were warned about the dangers of such false worship; the New Testament also warns against idolatry (1 Corinthians 10:14; Colossians 3:5; 1 John 5:21).

How foolish we can be as mortals, supposing that anything can compare to Jehovah. God himself poses the question in Isaiah 46:5, "To whom will you compare me or make me equal? Who will you measure me with, so that we should be like each other?" The answer is that there is no conjured-up deity that can ever compare to the one true God, no matter from what material they may be fashioned. Yet we still often foolishly place our trust in human-made objects, current projects, or important positions.

When we are tempted to place our trust in something—or someone—other than God, let's recall the ways he is unlike any other:

He is omnipotent—all-powerful.
He is omniscient—all-knowing.
He is omnipresent—present everywhere.
He is immutable—unchanging.

The God who created us, knitting us together in our mothers' wombs, is the only one who can carefully carry us until our days on earth are over. May we never foolishly place our trust in anything or anyone other than him.

POINTS TO PONDER

In what modern-day idols are you tempted to place your trust?

_____

_____

_____

_____

Why do you think you look to these human-made things instead of toward God?

_____

_____

_____

_____

_____

Father, *help me to be on guard against the idols I may be tempted to erect in my own life. May I ever be mindful that* _____

_____

_____

_____

77 | The Reward of Prayer

Ruth

Most often, when we think about prayer, it is easy to feel guilty! We might feel like we aren't praying as much as we should be. There are seasons when God seems distant. Or we feel dry. Our thoughts wander. We fall asleep. Maybe we feel like we don't pray the right way or experience God's presence like others do.

So we feel guilty when we think about getting alone with God. But our invitation to prayer is never meant to leave us feeling guilty; it is meant to lead us to appreciate the Gift—and to ground us in a life-giving relationship with Jesus.

The gift God gives us is the gift of himself. He feeds us and fuels us, enabling us to love him and love others well. It is easy to walk through life always reacting or responding to what is acting against us. And when we do that long enough, we no longer have anything to give others.

If prayer is communion with God, then Jesus' whole life was a prayer! In his life and ministry, we see what true prayer looks like—Jesus was always in communion and communication with the Father, in the power of the Holy Spirit.

This is why Jesus got alone (Mark 1:35). Later in Mark's gospel, we see another example: "After leaving them, he went up on a mountainside to pray" (Mark 6:46).

Our getting alone to pray is to meet with God. But it is never meant to be an end in and of itself. Jesus engages, disengages, and then reengages.

The reward is God himself, filling us and empowering us more and more to love him and sacrificially serve others.

So can solitude and silence be difficult? Can we struggle to pray? Absolutely. But living without prayer is even harder. Because living without prayer is really living apart from the life-giving relationship with God the Father, through Jesus, in the power of the Holy Spirit. His invitation to meet with him is not to guilt you, but to gift you. He wants to gift you with more of his grace and truth today. The reward is not what we get *from* him; the gift is the relationship we have *with* him.

POINTS TO PONDER

How has prayer made you feel guilty, and why?

_____

_____

_____

Our focus shouldn't necessarily be on prayer, but rather on the relationship God is inviting us into. The gift he wants to give us is the gift of himself. How can understanding this change the way you approach prayer?

_____

_____

_____

PAUSING TO PRAY

Father, I offer my heart to you. You are my reward. I confess, I have made prayer _____

_____

78 | The Ultimate Unfriending

Karen

Scripture to Study

Even my close friend in whom I trusted, who ate my bread, has lifted his heel against me.

Psalm 41:9 ESV

I love looking at old photographs, whether they are yellowing Polaroids from my childhood or snapshots of my three kids smiling up at me from the pages of their partially and pitifully finished scrapbooks. (I bought all the clever supplies but then only created a few pages!) Sometimes, however, a tiny pinch develops in my heart when I notice a picture of a certain friend from college.

This friend turned on me one day for reasons I never could figure out. And then they attempted to get others to turn on me! The sense of betrayal still bubbles up, feeling almost as fresh as it was all those years ago. Thankfully, I'm not alone in dealing with such emotions. The writer of Psalm 41, David, was also acquainted with the deceit and desertion of a friend.

We see David depict a person who is utterly unkind. Psalm 41:5 introduces the topic of David's enemies as he describes one who speaks "in malice." The Hebrew indicates injurious, harmful, and ethically evil speech. Such words of malice were not just uttered with the intent of being mean or critical; they were spoken with the goal of causing great harm to the person's heart and/or reputation.

A few verses later we are told that at least one of the people now numbered among David's enemies didn't start out that way. He was once in David's inner circle of friends: "Even my close friend in whom I trusted, who ate my bread, has lifted his heel against me." The phrase "lifted his heel" is an idiom first portrayed in Genesis 25:19–26, where the noun *heel* is coupled with the verb *deceive*. In the account of Rebekah giving birth to twins Esau and Jacob, the latter came out of the womb second with his brother's heel grasped firmly in his hand. Jacob became known for being a deceiver—tricking his brother into selling his birthright for a bowl of stew, and then deceiving his aged father, Isaac, by masquerading as Esau to steal his blessing.

Jesus had his own experience with this concept during the final days of his earthly life. On Jesus' last night with his friends, he announced that one of them would soon betray him by lifting his heel against him (John 13:18).

Have you had a falling-out with someone, leaving you with a now-fractured friendship? Do you wonder what you ever did to deserve such a change in treatment? Does this shift in your relationship pester your mind and threaten to eat away at your soul?

We aren't the only ones who have felt unfriended in life. May we take comfort in knowing that not only the psalmist David but the Lord Jesus himself also had friends who turned against them. Thankfully, we all have a Father who never leaves or forsakes us (Hebrews 13:5).

A faithful God trumps a fraudulent friend every single time.

POINTS TO PONDER

Have you ever suffered the sting of betrayal?

How can the words of Psalm 41 help you put the situation in proper perspective as you recall God's faithfulness in your life?

_____

_____

PAUSING TO PRAY

Father, thank you for remaining faithful even when others desert or despise me. And thank you for the ultimate act of friendship, your only Son, Jesus, who _____

79 | It's Okay to Rest

Ruth

Scripture to Study

Then he lay down under the bush and fell asleep.

1 Kings 19:5

When Elijah ran for his life after his confrontation with the prophets of Baal on Mount Carmel (1 Kings 18:16–46), he fled into the desert—that dry and hot and dangerous terrain of southern Israel, where things usually go to die, not live!

In Israel's history, it was a place of transition from an old life in Egypt to a new life in Canaan—the land of promise. It was also a place of testing. It was not usually a safe place, nor a place to be strengthened.

Yet throughout Israel's history, at different times and in different ways, it would be a place of rest. No place is off-limits for God's presence! And where God is present, among God's people, there is peace, protection, and provision. Our challenge often is seeing those places where God is inviting us to stop. To rest. And to be strengthened along the way.

Elijah would find such a spot when he fled into the desert. It would come in the form of a broom tree, also called a juniper. This shrub was nothing impressive. But when you are exhausted and fleeing for your life, which Elijah was, you aren't looking for impressive!

We're told that Elijah "lay down under the bush and fell asleep" (1 Kings 19:5). He was tired, worn out, and afraid. We're not told how long he was asleep, only that an angel finally woke him up, gave him food to eat, and then let him go back to sleep (vv. 5–6). Waking him up a second time, the angel gave him more food and drink because this "journey is too much" for Elijah (v. 7). We're then told that he was strengthened by his stopping, which enabled him to continue on his journey for forty days and forty nights (v. 8).

Maybe you are like me and you also would have run right by the broom tree! I wonder, as we struggle to walk by faith and trust God, how often we miss those little provisions in the desert. The shade of a broom tree. A walk. A short nap. Saying no to an ask. The small and simple stops our souls need to rest and be strengthened by God's presence.

POINTS TO PONDER

What are the "broom trees" God is asking you to stop and rest under to find strength?

_____

_____

Even when we stop, God does not. He is the God who does not sleep (Psalm 121:3–4) and sustains all things so we don't have to. How can truly understanding God's provision for you change the way you live day to day?

_____

_____

_____

_____

PAUSING TO PRAY

Father, I will find rest by _____

_____

80 | Lose the Fret; Keep the Faith

Karen

Scripture to Study

Do not be anxious about anything, but in everything by prayer and supplication with thanksgiving let your requests be made known to God.

Philippians 4:6 ESV

Years ago, I was part of an adult small group at church. After our study was finished each week, we'd spend time sharing any requests we had for prayer. Often, many requests were tethered to worry. A parent was worried about a wayward adult child. A young couple worried they might not be able to pay the rent that month. Another person was worried about a loved one who'd recently been diagnosed with a life-threatening disease.

Usually, just after the last request had been given and we were about to pray, one woman in our group would pipe up, uttering the same phrase each week: "Well, these things don't surprise God none. Let's all pray!" My Christian sister wasn't being flippant; she was sincere. She was also echoing a lesson we get from Scripture.

The apostle Paul doesn't merely tell the Philippians not to be anxious, but also instructs them what to do instead: "In everything by prayer and supplication with thanksgiving let your requests be made known to God."

Just what is the difference between prayer, supplication, and requests? Specific Greek words are used for each of these terms. Let's look at the middle word first, since it is the most common way we might think of prayer.

The word translated as "supplication" means seeking something you lack by asking for it or imploring God due to a serious individual need. The conversation is one-sided—you are doing the asking.

The word that is translated "prayer" means something slightly different. This term conveys more of an exchange, a conversation in which we are making pleas and also receiving an answer.

The word *requests* signifies a more formal petition. A petition is an official plea to an authority, asking for action in a case or situation.

And finally, let's not skip over the *way* in which we are to ask God—with thanksgiving.

When those elements are stitched altogether, we can think of it this way: We can initiate a dialogue with God wherever we may be. We converse with him, thanking him for all he has given to us and done for us. Our prayer time includes requests stemming from our deep personal needs and what we find lacking in our lives. But it shouldn't always be one-sided. We pray expecting God to answer. And we may also—as in a petition—give our reasons behind the requests. We are appealing to the ultimate Authority when we pray, knowing with confidence that he hears us.

Whatever is on your anxious heart today, remember that it doesn't surprise God one tiny bit. Take it to him now in prayer. The Lord is near. He will hear and answer.

May the Holy Spirit—our ultimate Helper—infuse you with the supernatural ability to lose the fret and keep the faith.

POINTS TO PONDER

Describe a situation in your life that is causing your heart to be anxious.

_____

_____

_____

_____

_____

_____

What specifically from this lesson defining three words in Philippians 4:6 can help to calm your fretful heart?

_____

_____

_____

_____

_____

_____

---- **PAUSING TO PRAY** ----

Dear Lord, _I am so grateful that you are bigger than any problem I face today. I ask for your help in_ _____

_____

_____

_____

81 | When People Let You Down

Ruth

Scripture to Study

When he rose from prayer and went back to the disciples, he found them asleep, exhausted from sorrow. "Why are you sleeping?" he asked them. "Get up and pray so that you will not fall into temptation."

Luke 22:45–46

Shortly before Jesus was arrested, he found himself alone—on purpose. Luke tells us that Jesus and his disciples went to the Mount of Olives, but upon arriving there, he "withdrew" (Luke 22:41). Or more literally, he tore himself away from his closest and dearest friends, the disciples.

The Greek word translated "withdrew" in Luke 22:41 is used in another place in the New Testament, when the apostle Paul is saying goodbye to his friends and the elders of the church in Ephesus. There, Luke says it this way: "After we had torn ourselves away from them, we put out to sea and sailed straight to Kos" (Acts 21:1).

Jesus' time had come, and the weight of what lay ahead was crushing. The severing or tearing away from even his closest friends to do the Father's will was painful. And yet it was necessary. The darkness that Jesus was experiencing, he was experiencing for us all. The Light was invading the darkness, and in his hour of prayer and preparation, even his closest of friends would fall asleep on him.

Luke goes on to tell us that when Jesus returned from praying, he found his closest of friends sleeping, not standing with him in prayer. He found them wiped out. Weary. Not terribly concerned or compassionate. So Jesus found himself alone. But this time, unlike the time of his own withdrawal, it was his closest friends who had withdrawn from him.

We don't read that Jesus was terribly offended or hurt, as we likely would be. Luke tells us, "When he rose from prayer and went back to the disciples, he found them asleep, exhausted from sorrow. 'Why are you sleeping?' he asked them. 'Get up and pray so that you will not fall into temptation'" (Luke 22:45–46). Instead of being wounded, Jesus simply warns them.

Although Jesus loved people, he didn't need people. Not like we do. He models for us the security of rooting our life in the Father's love while not relying on people. So if you feel like you have been let down, be careful of running from those who have fallen asleep on you. Instead, run to the love of our Father, who always loves perfectly. He is the God who never withdraws from us. Even the best of friends cannot love us like only he can.

POINTS TO PONDER

In what ways have you relied on people too much?

_____

_____

Our lives will never be marked by sacrificial love unless they are rooted in the Source of love. How can understanding this change the way you approach your friendships?

_____

_____

_____

PAUSING TO PRAY

Father, *fill me with the love you have for me. I confess that I have looked to others for* _____

82 | Praise Him Anyhow

Karen

Scripture to Study

I will tell of your name to my brothers; in the midst of the congregation I will praise you.

Psalm 22:22 ESV

When I was in high school, I attended the country church just across the road from my home. In that white clapboard building with the towering steeple, I soaked up all I could learn about the Bible each Sunday morning sitting in Miss Pat's class.

On the wall of the classroom was a poster that depicted a young boy with a slingshot in his back pocket and an ice cream cone in his hand. Unfortunately, his scoop of dairy delight had rolled off the cone and was being consumed by his puppy. The caption on the poster read, "Praise the Lord Anyhow."

Psalm 22 describes a suffering servant who chose to praise the Lord despite the enemies who threatened his life. As David's pen scrawled out a tale of both pain and praise in this portion of Scripture, several snippets give us a clue as to what situations and experiences in his own life he may have been referring. However, we will also see that, although this psalm was crafted by the former shepherd boy David, it is ultimately about a future event.

Most Bible scholars agree this psalm is not penned with only David's life in mind, but it is predominantly a prophetic foreshadowing of the sacrificial death of Jesus Christ. In the New Testament, Matthew 27:46 and Mark 15:34 each show Jesus quoting Psalm 22:1 on the cross when he uttered the Aramaic words, *"Eloi, Eloi, lema sabachthani?"* which means, "My God, my God, why have you forsaken me?"

Although both David and the Lord Jesus felt deserted and disowned, we still see a thread of preeminent praise during the emotional torture and physical pain. Praise pops off the page when, in the middle of this account in Psalm 22 (ESV) of being chased and tormented, David declares, "Yet you are holy" (v. 3). He also verbalizes God's steadfast care for him since his birth (vv. 9–10) and thanks God for being his rescuer (v. 21).

David vows to not only praise God despite his terrifying troubles but to speak God's name unashamedly in front of others. He praises God before the congregation and performs his vows before others who fear the Lord (vv. 22, 25).

As we look to the psalmist David and his writings, we are propelled forward in history's timeline to the greater David, Jesus himself—the sacrificial Savior who set for us the ultimate example of how to praise God even when life gets difficult and daunting.

May the examples of both David and Jesus inspire us to praise God no matter what we are experiencing. There isn't a crisis or concern with which Jesus cannot identify. He knows our situation and is waiting for us to take our worries and concerns to him.

Let's wrap our requests in a blanket of praise. Praise and panic cannot coexist. May any fear we are experiencing fizzle away as we choose to praise the Lord anyhow.

POINTS TO PONDER

Are you currently in a situation or season of life where you need to praise God despite your circumstances?

How do the words of Psalm 22 help you?

_____

_____

_____

_____

PAUSING TO PRAY

Father, *may I not allow the circumstances of my life to keep my lips tightly closed. I choose to praise you despite* _____

_____

_____

_____

_____

_____

_____

83 | Like a Child

Ruth

Scripture to Study

Truly I tell you, anyone who will not receive the kingdom of God like a little child will never enter it.

Luke 18:17

Recently, our youngest daughter stretched out on the couch next to me and laid her head on my lap. She needed to snuggle with her mama. As she creeps closer to her teenage years, the days of scooping her up in my arms as a baby or toddler are long gone. But one thing remains: her need to be close to me. To be loved and held. To be a child.

I cherish those snuggly moments with each of our kids, even though they are all too big to hold. And as I draped my arms next to her that afternoon, I wondered if we ever truly outgrow the desire to be a child. Are we really ever big enough or old enough to quiet the longing to be known, cherished, and cared for?

I am fascinated with how often Jesus spoke of children and even honored them and elevated them in ways that were uncommon at the time. He describes the disciples as "little children" (Matthew 18:14). He even says they are examples of what it looks like to belong and behave in God's kingdom.

People were also bringing babies to Jesus for him to place his hands on them. When the disciples saw this, they rebuked them. But Jesus called the children to him and said, "Let the little children come to me, and do not hinder them, for the kingdom of God belongs to such as these. Truly I tell you, anyone who will not receive the kingdom of God like a little child will never enter it."

Luke 18:15–17

As it turns out, we never do outgrow being a child. What we have to do, by God's grace, is grow into being a child—a spiritual son or daughter. It's a truth that by faith takes the help of God's Spirit to constantly remind us that we are his (Romans 8:14–17).

God sees you as his child. Do you really believe that you have a Father who cares for you and will provide for you? Our peace doesn't come from knowing God's plan; our peace comes from knowing God's heart. It is enough for a child to know he or she is loved. This is the heart of God for you right now. To rest in knowing that you are loved. You are his child, and everything is going to be okay.

POINTS TO PONDER

How can you focus more on God's heart instead of God's plan?

_____

_____

_____

Trust is not about knowing the future; trust is about knowing the heart of our Father. In what areas of your life do you need to come to him as a child, trusting he will take care of you?

_____

_____

_____

PAUSING TO PRAY

Father, *give me the grace to trust you with* _____

_____

84 | What We Do with Jesus

Karen

Scripture to Study

Pilate asked them, "What should I do then with Jesus, who is called Christ?"

Matthew 27:22 CSB

Recently, I saw a social media poll: "Who was the greatest human who ever lived?" The top ten responses ranged from the physicist Albert Einstein to U.S. President Abraham Lincoln to English playwright William Shakespeare. But one of the responses was Jesus Christ . . . coming in second to Mahatma Gandhi.

I was a little aggravated. Not because Jesus was awarded the runner-up trophy but because he was even in the poll results! After all, the question was, "Who was the greatest *human* who ever lived?" While Jesus was fully human, he was also fully God.

People often think of Jesus as *only* a great human being or a superior moral teacher, ranking him alongside founders of other prominent world religions. And yet another segment of society dubs him the greatest conman who ever lived, as though he amassed a following by false declarations of divinity.

Our thoughts about Jesus and his claims spill over into our actions because what we think *about* Jesus determines what we do *with* him.

In the book of Matthew, Pilate, the governor of Judea, addresses a gathering crowd. He poses an important question that explores not only what the crowd thinks about Jesus but what they want done with him: "Pilate asked them, 'What should I do then with Jesus, who is called Christ?'" (Matthew 27:22).

The crowd cried out for Jesus to be crucified. To them, he was an offender of the Law who must be done away with immediately.

The leading religious leaders had him captured and killed (Matthew 26:3–4). Judas Iscariot betrayed him (Matthew 26:14–16). The soldiers in attendance mocked him (Matthew 27:27–31). Bystanders misunderstood him when he tried to speak from the cross (Matthew 27:47).

However, not all reacted to him adversely. Some women brought spices and perfume to the grave and were the first to announce the news that Christ had risen from the dead (Luke 23:55–56; 24:1–12). And the centurion who witnessed the death of Jesus had perhaps the most accurate view of Jesus. This centurion cried out, "Truly this man was the Son of God!" (Matthew 27:50–54 CSB).

Isn't it amazing that people can come to such different conclusions in their thinking about one single soul? But as interesting as it is to ponder their varied responses, the most important question this side of eternity is this:

What will *we* do with Jesus?

Will we be content to keep him nonchalantly grouped with other "good teachers" who urge love, good deeds, and peace on earth? Might we possibly misunderstand Christ, never having taken the time to study who he really is? Or do we ignore him altogether, leaving him tucked away inside the pages of the Bible but sadly absent from our day-to-day lives?

Here is what we *can* do with Jesus: Believe who *he* says he is. Trust him in all the things and allow him to change our hearts. Proclaim him to everyone. Never back down when following him becomes difficult and costly.

Just what will *you* do with Jesus? Your answer is perhaps the most important one you will ever give.

POINT TO PONDER

If someone were to ask you to describe Jesus, who would you say he is to you?

_____

_____

PAUSING TO PRAY

Father, *please help me to act in a way that accurately depicts who you are. You are not merely a moral, historical person. You most certainly are* _____

_____

_____

_____

_____

85 | Not Enough Time

Ruth

Scripture to Study

The world and its desires pass away, but whoever does the will of God lives forever.

1 John 2:17

There's just not enough time. I often feel this way about a day or a week or month. Even a year can slip by and I'll realize I didn't do all I wanted to or even planned to do! Have you ever felt that way? It can feel like there is just too much to do and too little time to do it.

The struggle is real, and what we do with time is incredibly important. As it turns out, even our time, which is a gift, is not outside of God's plans and purposes for us. After all, he is the One who gives us each day. He is the One who created us and is now sustaining us. He is the One who has gifted us. And he is the One who has called us into a relationship with Jesus and called us each uniquely to serve him.

So the question is, what will we do with our time?

The Bible reminds us that not only is time limited, but time can be squandered. Time can be wasted. Misused. One example is in 1 John 2:17, where we are told that, "The world and its desires pass away, but whoever does the will of God lives forever."

"The world," John writes, and its "desires" are going to come to an end. They will be brought to nothing. All of the values and ambitions that the world is chasing after and spending so much time to possess will come to nothing before God one day. Not only the treasure of the world, but all the time spent pursuing that treasure, will be shown for what it is.

But the one who pursues the things of God? The one who does God's will? They will live forever. They will see God and enjoy him with no end! Time will never take away that treasure.

How are you spending your time? Where we spend our time often reflects what our treasure is.

POINTS TO PONDER

How can you build your time around your treasure?

_____

_____

_____

_____

We can get a more accurate picture of what we have made more important than doing God's will by looking at our schedules. Take some time to look at your schedule this week and identify one simple way you can adjust your time to reflect God's desires and not your own.

_____

_____

_____

_____

PAUSING TO PRAY

Father, show me what you are calling me to in this season. My time reveals that I have _____

_____

86 | Believing Is Seeing

Karen

Scripture to Study

Jesus said, "Because you have seen me, you have believed. Blessed are those who have not seen and yet believe."

John 20:29 CSB

It was time to get our elementary and middle school-aged children ready to go to a graduation open house. These parties are huge deals in my area of the country. Family, friends, co-workers, and neighbors drop by to enjoy a buffet of food complete with cake piled with thick frosting in the student's school colors. We also play lawn games, have bonfires, and congratulate the guest of honor on completing thirteen years of school. Since these celebrations are such a blast, I couldn't figure out why our middle child was reluctant to go.

I asked what his hesitancy was. Instead of giving me a straight answer, he began to interrogate me with a long list of questions: Who all was going to be there? Would his friend Johnny already be there when we arrived? What food would they have to eat? Who would he sit by when eating? Were the kids going to play flag football and if so, would they let him be the quarterback?

This inquisitive child had an unrelenting desire to know exactly how things would transpire at any social event before he became excited about going. Naturally, I was not able to answer all his inquiries. So I turned the tables on him by tossing out my own question. "Well, I can't tell you exactly how everything will go, but I'm sure that if you look for it, you will find fun. Can you think of an open house we have gone to as a family where you didn't find something delicious to eat and someone you enjoyed hanging out with?"

Eventually he agreed that he always did end up having a great time. He knew he could trust our promise of fun, even if he wouldn't know all the details beforehand. Sometimes, riveting your mind on what you do know helps your heart to deal with what you don't.

In the book of John, we see a large crowd following Jesus because they saw the signs he was performing (John 6:2). Throughout the Gospels, Christ was able to draw a following when his actions were spectacular and miraculous. To the people, seeing was believing. Yet Jesus argues that an upside-down truth is more desirable: Those who have not seen and yet already believe are blessed—a term that means happy, fortunate, and to be envied.

Do we only follow Jesus when we see signs that he is working, or do we trust him when we don't see any evidence of his movement? If he is the Alpha and Omega—the A and the Z—can we trust him with the L-M-N-O-P, the in-between things we don't know? (Okay, that was weird. Spellcheck corrected L-M-N-O-P to the word *omnipotent*, meaning unlimited in power and able to do anything!)

Life is not steeped in certitude. Will you dare to trust God even when you don't know all the details of what lies ahead? When we choose to believe, we will see his steadfast love and gentle care for us unfold.

Even at those times when we can't understand his actions—or his seeming silence—we can still choose to trust his heart.

POINTS TO PONDER

In what life situation(s) are you dying to know all the details of what lies ahead?

_____

_____

_____

_____

_____

What can you do to show God that you trust him to have your best interests at heart, regardless of what the future holds in this area?

_____

_____

_____

_____

_____

_____

PAUSING TO PRAY

Father God, *when I can't sense you working, help me to remember*

_____

_____

_____

_____

87 | Painful Partings

Ruth

Scripture to Study

He withdrew about a stone's throw beyond them, knelt down and prayed.

Luke 22:41

We were made for relationships. Meaningful friendships. The kind of community that is marked by sacrificial love, humility, and intimacy. The kind of community that reflects the very character of God as Father, Son, and Spirit.

And yet, what makes relationships so powerful is the same thing that makes relationships so painful when they are severed. We lose the intimate bond and self-giving love we once enjoyed. The deeper the friendship, the deeper the hurt. This is the challenge of not only loving deeply, but at different times and in different ways, also loving freely.

Sometimes it is a friend who moves to a new city or state.

A friend changes jobs. Or maybe switches churches.

There are those times when misunderstanding, hurt, or offense takes its toll.

All of these changes can cause separation. A severing that is painful. But there is another kind of separation that can be necessary in our lifelong journey of trust in Jesus.

This separation occurs when we change, and there is a deepening of our conversation—a deepening in our desire to walk closer to God. Such a change requires a "withdrawal" in order to do the will of God in some area of our life.

In those times when we change, the relationship changes as a result. The separation comes when our growing closer to Jesus requires growing further away from a friend. The severing is necessary for our sanctification.

This happened to me when I first became a Christian. It didn't last forever. And it didn't happen in all my relationships. But I had a choice to make, a difficult one that caused me to distance myself for a time from friends who were not pursuing Jesus with me, nor were they promoting Jesus in me.

It's interesting that Jesus, just before he was arrested, had to withdraw even from his closest friends, the disciples. It wasn't that they were a bad influence. It was necessary for him to do so in preparation to draw near to his Father and do his will. As we saw earlier, in devotion 81, "When People Let You Down," the word translated "withdrew" is even stronger in Greek, literally meaning to be "torn away."

Our greatest joy is in walking closely with God. And at different times in our surrender to him, this means a withdrawal from someone or something that is standing in the way of greater intimacy and greater obedience. Who or what is God asking you to consider withdrawing from? Remember when he does this that it is not to steal life, but to give more life to us!

POINTS TO PONDER

Who or what is God asking you to withdraw from and why?

_____

We were made for community. So how can distancing ourselves from certain relationships actually deepen our relationship with Christ?

_____

_____

PAUSING TO PRAY

Father, *I desire to deepen my relationship with you by* _____

_____

88 | On Wailing and Worship

Karen

Scripture to Study

But the hour is coming, and is now here, when the true worshipers will worship the Father in spirit and truth, for the Father is seeking such people to worship him. God is spirit, and those who worship him must worship in spirit and truth.

John 4:23–24 ESV

One day at high noon, a woman from Samaria went to draw water from what was known as Jacob's well, when she encountered Jesus. He asked her for a drink. Their conversation soon pivoted from speaking of actual water to talking about living water and eternal life. She became so intrigued by what Jesus was telling her that she asked him to get her some of that living water so she would never thirst again.

Of course, the Lord didn't grab a bucket and lower it down for some liquid refreshment. Instead, he began to talk to her about her life, including the fact that she'd had several husbands and was now living with a man to whom she was not married. His keen insight into her life situation—seemingly without having any prior knowledge—caused her to believe she was talking to a prophet. Well, if there's a prophet standing in front of you, you're going to seize the opportunity to ask any questions you might have, right?

So she asked Jesus a question about worship. She wondered if she should worship on the mountain where her ancestors did, or in Jerusalem where others said was proper. And I just love Jesus' answer to her. He replied, "God is spirit, and those who worship him must worship in spirit and truth" (John 4:24 ESV).

The Greek word used here for spirit is *pneúma* and means "spirit (Spirit), wind, or breath."[1] (It might make you think of the word *pneumonia*, which is an inflammation of the lungs' air sacs that makes it hard for a person to breathe.) The most frequent translation of *pneúma* in the New Testament is written with a capital S—Spirit—meaning the Holy Spirit.

The Greek word for truth is *alétheia*. This word indicates that which is honest, sincere, and straightforward. When we crochet worshiping in spirit together with being entirely truthful, we get two actions that—although they seem opposite—intertwine perfectly together . . .

Wailing and worship.

Wailing and worship hold hands. Not just in the Bible, but they can in our lives today.

True worshipers, Jesus claimed, worship both in spirit and in truth. We can worship God through the power of the Holy Spirit, reading, praying, or singing, at times being struck with his awe. We worship in trust, recognizing that God is God and—news flash—we are not! We must allow the Lord to call the shots in our life. But this is no candy-coated worship, full of religious-sounding words and cliché spiritual phrases. No, we can be honest, candid, and straightforward with God, even going so far as to lament and wail, telling the Lord about the good, the bad, and the oh-so-ugly in our lives.

Pour your heart out to Jesus—raw emotions and all. But once you have uttered that final "Amen," quietly trust the outcome, knowing that God knows so much better than we do just what is best for us.

POINTS TO PONDER

In what ways might wailing and worship hold hands in time spent alone with God?

_____

_____

_____

List one concern you currently have along with two worship-worthy attributes of God.

_____

_____

_____

Gracious Father, I want to worship you in spirit and in truth. Empower me to _____

_____

_____

_____

_____

89 | Giving God Your Past

Ruth

Scripture to Study

He withdrew about a stone's throw beyond them, knelt down and prayed.

Luke 22:41

Some people worry about their future. And then there are others who are haunted by their past. But the good news of God's love and forgiveness in Jesus is that both the past and the future have been dealt with by Jesus on the cross.

The bad news is quite simple. As we look in the rearview mirror of our lives, we all see the mistakes of trying to do life on our own terms. We see the sin of others, but we also see our own sin. We see the pain and hurt it caused us, and in many cases, the mark it left on others too.

The sin of our past, the things we've done and said, can haunt us. We may struggle with whether or not we are truly forgiven. Or if in some way, God is mad at us—punishing us, even. Back to the good news, though, that the cross has dealt with our past. Out of love for us, Jesus went to the cross so that we might be forgiven—so that we might have the most important relationship reconciled through repentance and faith in Jesus.

We are saved by grace—it is a free gift (Ephesians 2:8–9). We don't earn it. We don't deserve it. But because of God's mercy, he has made a way for our future to be different from our past. Jesus' work on the cross, and our faith in him, offers us the hope of a new life and new future!

If we trust God with our future, though, we need to trust him with our past.

In Romans 5:8, the apostle Paul reminds us that "God demonstrates his own love for us in this: While we were still sinners, Christ died for us." He goes on to say in verse 9, "Since we have now been justified by his blood, how much more shall we be saved from God's wrath through him!" In other words, the work of Jesus on the cross has saved us in the past and will save us in the future.

Have you received this good news? Has there been a time when you have said yes to Jesus? If you have already, is there is a part of your past that haunts you? Jesus is reminding you to give him not only your future, but to give him your past. The cross really was enough for both!

POINTS TO PONDER

What part(s) of your past are you holding on to and why?

_____

_____

_____

Struggling with our past can actually be a form of pride. How? Because we are believing that somehow what we have done is too great for God to forgive! In what area(s) of your life are you believing this lie today?

_____

_____

_____

PAUSING TO PRAY

Father, I have given you my future, now help me give you _____

_____

_____

90 | Learning to Live in a World without Why

Karen

Scripture to Study

O my God, I cry by day, but you do not answer,
and by night, but I find no rest.

Psalm 22:2 esv

Over the last two years I have experienced many instances of stress, sorrow, and grief. I lost two uncles, an aunt, two cousins, one of my son's childhood close friends, my stepmother, my father, and my mother all within that time frame. We also moved to a new town at the beginning of that two years to be close to all the grandparents on my side of the family, the very relatives who began dying just three weeks after we moved.

Mixed in among the grief and the stress of a move, we had occasions of joy. Our son got married to a wonderful woman from the Deep South he met through my Instagram account. Our daughter also became a Mrs. at the very beginning of the COVID crisis, getting hitched in my friends' backyard after travel shutdowns canceled the family-only destination wedding in Spain we were planning. Oh, and yes, nearly all of this happened during the first eighteen months of the pandemic.

While trying my best to navigate all of this, I found myself almost behaving like a toddler following around his or her parents, uttering that one-syllable word repeatedly with each new situation they encounter: "Why?"

Why did God seem to direct us to a brand-new town just ten minutes from all my kids' grandparents if they were all going to pass away so shortly after we moved? Why did our son's friend die from an overdose the very first time she dabbled in drugs? Why did a cousin of mine have to bury her mother while almost simultaneously burying her husband, nearly collapsing under the weight of such grief? And of course, probably all of us wonder why this dangerous and disruptive pandemic had to hit.

I take comfort in knowing the writers of the Psalms often lamented, wrestling with questions of why and expressing deep grief. In Psalm 22:2 we read the relentless begging to God for answers, even when none was anywhere in sight:

> O my God, I cry by day, but you do not answer,
> and by night, but I find no rest.

I wish I had a slick, easy formula for learning to live in a world without the answers. Unfortunately, I don't. But I have seen some benefits of dwelling in the space between the now and the not yet—that future time when we will no longer wonder but will dwell in a place without sorrow or tears.

I've learned that not knowing why pushes me harder into God's Word. It makes me long to cling to the Lord like nothing else. It grants me deep empathy for others who are also navigating a life without answers. In short, living in a world without why forces me to lean on Jesus with every ounce of my resolve.

Might we be bold enough to trade in our *why* for a *Who*? May we stop putting so much emphasis on the unanswered questions. Instead, let's seek a closer walk with the One who can sustain us even though our whys linger.

POINTS TO PONDER

In what situation(s) in life are you continually asking God why?

_____

_____

How can the words of Psalm 22:2 comfort you, knowing people have struggled since Old Testament times with wondering why?

_____

_____

_____

_____

_____

_____

PAUSING TO PRAY

Dear God, *although there are still so many unanswered questions, from now on I want to learn* _____

_____

_____

_____

_____

ACKNOWLEDGMENTS

To our friend and agent Meredith Brock for believing in us and this project. We wouldn't want to do ministry with anybody else.

To Jennifer Dukes Lee and our Bethany House Publishers family for partnering with us to encourage others to trust God in every area of life. Your hard work and prayers mean the world to us.

To our countless friends—both in real life and online—who encourage us daily and help us to follow hard after God, trusting him in all the things.

To our families for their endless support and willingness to chip in around the house as we worked on this manuscript. Our love for you knows no bounds.

And finally, to our Lord and Savior Jesus Christ, for the indescribable gift of salvation. What an immense honor it is to serve you.

NOTES

Introduction

1. "Calm," *Cambridge Dictionary*, (Cambridge University Press, 2021). Accessed September 8, 2021, https://dictionary.cambridge.org/us/dictionary/english/calm.

8. A Sermonette for Your Soul

1. "5315. nephesh," *Strong's Concordance*, Biblehub.com. Accessed August 19, 2021, https://biblehub.com/hebrew/5315.htm.

14. A Peace That's Out of This World

1. "2889. kosmos," *Strong's Concordance*, Biblehub.com. Accessed August 19, 2021, https://biblehub.com/greek/2889.htm.

18. Successful or Suffering?

1. "3986. Peirasmos," *Strong's Concordance*, Biblehub.com. Accessed August 18, 2021, https://biblehub.com/greek/3986.htm.

22. Following from Close Behind

1. "1692. Dabaq," *Strong's Concordance*, Biblehub.com. Accessed August 20, 2021, https://biblehub.com/hebrew/1692.htm.
2. "310. achar," *Strong's Concordance*, Biblehub.com. Accessed August 20, 2021, https://biblehub.com/hebrew/310.htm.

32. Just Keep Moving

1. "2570. kalos," *Strong's Concordance*, Bible Hub. Accessed, August 19, 2021, https://biblehub.com/greek/2570.htm.

34. On Stashing and Storing

1. "6845. tsaphan," *Strong's Concordance*, Bible Hub. Accessed August 19, 2021, https://biblehub.com/hebrew/6845.htm.

40. Drop the Security Blanket

1. "5399. phobeó," *Thayer's Greek Lexicon*, Bible Hub. Accessed August 19, 2021, https://biblehub.com/greek/5399.htm.
2. "5399. phobeó," *Thayer's*.

88. On Wailing and Worship

1. "4151. pneuma," *Strong's Concordance*, Bible Hub. Accessed August 24, 2021, https://biblehub.com/greek/4151.htm.

Karen Ehman is a *New York Times* bestselling author of eighteen books and a writer for Proverbs 31 Ministries *Encouragement for Today,* an online devotional that reaches over four million women daily. She is married to her college sweetheart and is the mother of five kids—three biological and two by marriage, although she forgets which ones are which. She resides in rural Mid-Michigan. Connect with her at KarenEhman.com.

Ruth Schwenk is the founder of the popular blog *TheBetterMom.com,* and co-founder with her husband, Patrick, of the podcast *Rootlike Faith.* She is the author of several books, including *In a Boat in the Middle of a Lake,* co-authored with Patrick, as well as her bestselling devo, *The Better Mom Devotional.* Ruth lives with her husband and their four kids in the dreamy college town of Ann Arbor, Michigan.

Proverbs 31
M I N I S T R I E S

Know the Truth. Live the Truth. It changes everything.

If you were inspired by *Trusting God in All the Things* and desire to deepen your own personal relationship with Jesus Christ, Proverbs 31 Ministries has just what you are looking for.

Proverbs 31 Ministries exists to be a trusted friend who will take you by the hand and walk by your side, leading you one step closer to the heart of God through:

- Free online daily devotions
- First 5 Bible study app
- Online Bible Studies
- Podcast
- COMPEL Writer Training
- She Speaks Conference
- Books and resources

Our desire is to help you to know the Truth and live the Truth. Because when you do, it changes everything.

For more information about Proverbs 31 Ministries,
visit www.Proverbs31.org.